BEST PRACTICE

Process Management Based on SqEME®

SqEME Edition 2008

empowered by SqEME®

Constitution:
What are the essential characteristics of the enterprise?

Constitution

Enterprise architecture · Key result areas

Chemistry:
What makes it tick?
How does the energy flow?

Chemistry

Messages · Preconditions

Correspondence

Performances · Processes

Construction

People · Resources

Correspondence:
How have we performed in carrying out our business??

Construction:
How have we facilitated the work in the organization?

VHP

VAN HAREN PUBLISHING

Other publications by Van Haren Publishing

Van Haren Publishing (VHP) specializes in titles on Best Practices, methods and standards within IT management. Architecture (Enterprise and IT, business management and project management.

These publications are grouped in the series, eg: *ITSM Library* (on behalf of ITSMF International), *Best Practice* and *IT Management Topics*. VHP is also publisher on behalf of leading companies and institutions, eg The Open Group, IPMA-NL, CA, Getronics, Pink Elephant). At the time of going to press the following books are available:

IT (Service) Management / IT Governance
ITSM, ITIL® V3 and ITIL® V2
Foundations of IT Service Management – based on ITIL® V3
  (English, Dutch, German; French, Japanese and Spanish editions: Spring 2008)
Introduction to IT Service Management (ITIL V3, English)
IT Service Management based on ITIL V3 – A Pocket Guide
  (English, Dutch, German, Italian; French, Japanese and Spanish editions: Spring 2008)
Foundations of IT Service Management based on ITIL® (ITIL V2),
  (English, Dutch, French, German, Spanish, Japanese, Chinese, Danish, Italian, Korean, Russian, Arabic; also available as a CD-ROM)
Implementing Service and Support Management Processes (English)
Release and Control for IT Service Management, based on ITIL® - A Practitioner Guide (English)

ISO/IEC 20000
ISO/IEC 20000 – An Introduction
  (English, German: Spring 2008)
Implementing ISO/IEC 20000 Certification (English: Spring 2008)
ISO/IEC 20000 - A Pocket Guide (English, Italian, German, Spanish, Portuguese)

ISO 27001 and ISO 17799
Information Security based on ISO 27001 and ISO 17799 - A Management Guide (English)
Implementing Information Security based on ISO 27001 and ISO 17799 - A Management Guide (English)

CobiT
IT Governance based on CobiT4.1® - A Management Guide
  (English, German)

IT Service CMM
IT Service CMM - A Pocket Guide (English)

ASL and BiSL
ASL - A Framework for Application Management
  (English, German)
ASL - Application Services Library - A Management Guide
  (English, Dutch)
BiSL - A Framework for Business Information Management
  (Dutch, English)
BiSL - Business information Services Library - A Management Guide
  (Dutch; English)

ISPL
IT Services Procurement op basis van ISPL (Dutch)
IT Services Procurement based on ISPL – A Pocket Guide (English)

Other IT Management titles:
De RfP voor IT-outsourcing
  (Dutch; English version due Spring 2008)
Decision- en Controlfactoren voor IT-Sourcing (Dutch)
Defining IT Success through the Service Catalogue (English)
Frameworks for IT Management - An introduction (English, Japanese; German)
Frameworks for IT Management – A Pocket Guide
  (English, German, Dutch)
Implementing IT Governance (English)
Implementing leading standards for IT management
  (English, Dutch)
IT Service Management global best practices, volume (English)
IT Service Management Best Practices, volumes 1, 2, 3 and 4
  (Dutch)

ITSM from hell! / ITSM from hell based on Not ITIL (English)
ITSMP - The IT Strategy Management Process (English)
Metrics for IT Service Management (English, Russian)
Service Management Process Maps (English)
Six Sigma for IT Management (English)
Six Sigma for IT Management – A Pocket Guide (English)

MOF/MSF
MOF - Microsoft Operations Framework, A Pocket Guide
  (Dutch, English, French, German, Japanese)
MSF - Microsoft Solutions Framework, A Pocket Guide
  (English, German)

Architecture (Enterprise and IT)
TOGAF, The Open Group Architecture Framework – A Management Guide (English)
The Open Group Architecture Framework – 2007 Edition
  (English, official publication of TOG)
TOGAF™ Version 8 Enterprise Edition – Study Guide
  (English, official publication of TOG)
TOGAF™ Version 8.1.1 Enterprise Edition –A Pocket Guide
  (English, official publication of TOG)

Business Management
ISO 9000
ISO 9001:2000 - The Quality Management Process (English)

EFQM
The EFQM excellence model for Assessing Organizational Performance – A Management Guide (English)

SqEME®
Process management based on SqEME® (English)
SqEME® – A Pocket Guide (English, Dutch, mid 2008)

Project/Programme/Risk Management
ICB/NCB
NCB Versie 3– Nederlandse Competence Baseline
  (Dutch, on behalf of IPMA-NL)
Projectmanagement op basis van NCB V3 - IPMA-C en IPMA-D
  (Dutch)

PRINCE2™
Project Management based on PRINCE2™- Edition 2005
  (English, Dutch, German)
PRINCE2™ - A No Nonsense Management Guide (English)
PRINCE2™ voor opdrachtgevers – Management Guide (Dutch)

MINCE®
MINCE® – A Framework for Organizational Maturity (English)

MSP
Programme Management based on MSP (English, Dutch)
Programme Management based on MSP - A Management Guide
  (English)

M_o_R
Risk Management based on M_o_R - A Management Guide
  (English)

Other publications on project management:
Wegwijzer voor methoden bij Projectvolwassenheid
  (Dutch: fall 2008)
Het Project Management Office – Management Guide (Dutch)

For the latest information on VHP publications, visit our website: www.vanharen.net

Process Management Based on SqEME®
2008 Edition

A HORIZONTAL APPROACH TO ORGANIZING THE ENTERPRISE

www.sqeme.org

Edited by Jos.N.A. van Oosten

Colophon

Title:	Process Management Based on SqEME®, 2008 edition
A Publication of:	The SqEME Foundation (www.sqeme.org)
Publisher:	Van Haren Publishing (www.vanharen.net)
ISBN:	978 90 8753 136 2
Edition:	First edition, first impression, April 2008
Layout and design:	CO2 Premedia, Amersfoort-NL
Edited by:	Jos.N.A. van Oosten, Q-TIPS B.V. (www.q-tips.nl)
Translation:	Marcel F. Captijn, Technisch Tekstwerk Steve Newton
Copyright:	2008 The SqEME Foundation

Preface

Process Management based on SqEME® is an open standard for developing a processed centred architecture of an enterprise. It may be reproduced freely by any organization wishing to use it to develop a governance structure on the quality of their business processes.

The twentieth century view at organizing has passed its expiry date. The classic way of thinking went past the fact that organizations are open systems and are part of complex network structures. Processes have to hold a prominent place in observing organizations: how are the different parts of the organization tuned to each other and how does the messaging in between take place? SqEME® Process Management is a method that enables discussing the design of the organization in a subtle but unambiguous way.
SqEME® as a methodology views processes from four different perspectives. SqEME® calls this windows, by means of which one seeks for the Constitution, Chemistry, Correspondence and Construction of the enterprise. Looking through these windows is perceiving organizations in a different way. One not longer just sees the vertical lines of the hierarchic structure, but also (and particularly) the processes in the organization. This provides more insight in the organization, the 'horizontal organization', and gives the answer to the question of how to deal with IT today and how to get the maximum benefit from it.

For many years, SqEME® has been applied successfully in industry (chemistry, automotive, construction, paper), in the business sector (IT service, healthcare), in the non profit sector and in public companies such as the Prosecution Counsel, County Councils and local authorities. *Process Management based on SqEME®* abundantly draws on this experience and supplies the reader with all necessary grip to apply the method himself.

This book is especially meant for all professionals involved in the change process towards process-driven organizations. It is written in a way that all wanting to familiarize with process centred thinking will find an innovative, yet practice-proven approach in it.

This book is the result of experience with the management of business processes in various organizations over more than twenty years. A period of time during which successful results have been achieved by following an approach that over the years has become known under the name SqEME® Process Management. Time and time again, the positive effects of SqEME® Process Management have proved themselves in industry (chemical, automotive, construction, paper), in the commercial sector (including ICT service), in health care (also extramural health care) and in the non-profit sector, such as the Dutch Police Force, the Public Prosecutor and other governmental authorities.

SqEME® Process Management is a contemporary way of managing processes. The SqEME® method helps the reader to recognize, design, control, manage and improve processes in their own organization and supplies a set of consistent and coherent modelling techniques. In addition, and importantly, SqEME® Process Management is a methodology, so as well as being a way of observing processes in organizations, it provides an indication of how to do this. A key assumption in this method is the professional maturity of the employee. The focus is not on what the employee has to do in detail, but on the surrounding system. It is on cooperation and the flow of information between employees. 'SqEME®' organizations are agile and innovative, and they pay attention to craftsmanship, creativity and passion where it concerns their trade. 'SqEME®' organizations have room for dialogue, openness, interest and respect, whilst the eye remains focussed upon cooperative performance and achieving results.

From 1997 onwards, a network of private and public organizations, consultancy agencies and independent advisors has grown. Experiences in applying the method are discussed and insights into the basic assumptions and backgrounds are shared (see website www.sqeme.org). In 2002, the earlier Dutch version of this book was issued, supported by the network. Since then, it has provided firm support during SqEME® training sessions and reorganization projects in many organizations.

The first and the second edition of this book have both generated a lot of response. People who wished to be kept informed of the latest developments, or who have become members of the network or have supplied their feedback on the content. The establishment of the SqEME® Foundation at the end of 2006 is of particular significance. Our feeling is that the network has moved a further step towards maturity, especially in the way that the 'togetherness' and the open distribution of the method have been emphasized. The time has come for a third and completely revised edition which is with the release of this version also available in English. From this year on, 2008, the Board of the SqEME Foundation has even agreed on using the English language as the basic language for SqEME® Process Management.

SqEME® Process Management is being developed continuously and is being adapted to reflect recent developments. Practical experience remains the core. Experience from daily practice serves as an input for sharpening and developing the method. The growing domain of application of the method thus provides an increasing number of new insights. These have lead to adaptations of the book in this third and completely revised edition. The first and the second edition focused mainly on the method. This edition pays more attention to its application and the impact that it has upon the people working with the processes of the organization. SqEME® Process Management can be regarded as a 'business excellence' approach. It helps the reader to organize and improve the quality of business management. It offers a unique way to look at management of one's own company. In our opinion, this way of looking is a translation of how we organize work nowadays, from the present context and within the existing preconditions.

Contents

About the SqEME Foundation

The SqEME Foundation facilitates the development and the free dissemination of knowledge to all organizations and people who are committed to Process Management, based on SqEME.

By their membership, users of the SqEME® framework form a network organization. The SqEME Foundation works with 'end-users' of the SqEME® framework, business consultants and consultancy firms, training organizations, IT-suppliers and suppliers of Business Process Modelling Tools. Within this market place the SqEME Foundation is vendor-neutral. Its role is to capture, understand and share current and emerging utilizations of process management and process architectures to improve the performance of organizations.

The SqEME Foundation is the guardian of the basic concept which are stated in the first chapters of this book, shortly addressed as the use of the four windows and open and well defined standards for modelling processes.

The members of the board of the SqEME Foundation are delegates from the associated partner organizations. One board member is chosen by the members of the network to represent the interests of the network as a whole.

The SqEME Foundation and its associated members have over 20 years of experience in field of process management, the use of its concepts, the training of the principles, competences and skills. The SqEME Foundation develops and operates certification programs to validate conformance to open standards and specifications on the era of process management competences and process architectures.

Further information on the SqEME Foundation and the activities of the network organization is available at www.sqeme.org.

Trademarks

SqEME® is a trademark of the SqEME Foundation.

TOGAF™ and Boundaryless Information Flow™ are trademarks of The Open Group.

The SqEME Foundation acknowledges that there may be other company names and products that might be covered by trademark protection and advises the reader to verify them independently.

Acknowledgements

Ren Hilverdink, to whom this book is dedicated, is the founder of what is the mental legacy now named SqEME®. A group of enthusiastic people, gathered in the network of the SqEME foundation, have further developed and propagated it.

The original Dutch version of this book is written by five authors:

- In their consultancy work at Q-TIPS, Jos van Oosten, René van Velzen and Peter de Klein support managers discovering the business processes and improving the quality of the organization.
- Theo Snijders is an Organization Psychologist and works as an advisor in the area of organization issues and communication.
- Teun Hardjono, member of the prestigious International Academy for Quality and initiator and chairman of the Dutch Academy for Quality, combines over thirty years practice as an organization advisor with a professorship at the RSM Erasmus University Rotterdam. He holds a chair in Quality Management and Certification, established by the *Raad voor Accreditatie* (Dutch Accreditation Council) and mainly concentrates on organization design and organizational change.

Special words of thank are expressed to Frans Stevens for his contributions to, and feedback on previous versions of this book.

Last but not least many thanks to Marcel Captijn, Steve Newton, Arnold Mol, Jac Rongen, Huib van der Meijden, Stephan Bottemanne, Gerrit Laurenssen, Stuart Boardman, Maarten Meijer Cluwen, Ary Stigter, Peter van Dusseldorp for participating in the process of translating the SqEME® framework.

Jos. N.A. van Oosten
Everdingen-NL, March 16th 2008

Introduction

This book is about the SqEME® approach to process management. More and more organizations are discovering the 'phenomenon' of process management, and are either applying it or are planning to do so. Developments in the ICT area, the renewed attention for the 'professional' on the work-floor, external pressure through standards or legislation, and the necessity for more flexible ways of organizing are all contributing to this. But what does process management mean precisely? How do you make it specific? How can you involve the various units of the organization with process management? How do you use process models and process descriptions in an optimal way? Who are process owners and how can they be assigned or committed? And, above all, what use is it for the organization?

This book challenges and supplies the means to look at organizations in a different way. No longer along the lines of the hierarchical structures, but by focussing upon the processes in the organization. This book is primarily intended for anyone involved in the process of change towards process driven organizations. It is written in a manner that anyone wanting to familiarize themselves with process centred thinking will find an innovative yet proven approach.

This book originates from the domain of quality management but now focuses on the quality of the organization: how to let the enterprise achieve its business goals through a controlled organization which is fit for use? Experience suggests that the reasons to consider the quality of the organization via the means of process management can be found in the desire to:
• emphasize horizontal work flows within and between organizations;
• document processes, for example for the benefit of certification;
• avoid bureaucracy and unnecessary detail;
• develop and implement new information systems;
• strive for a more professional organization;
• realize transparency in the organization, e.g. to enable corporate governance;
• improve cooperation and utilize network structures;
• design an alternative for organizing according to the 'functional school' or 'Taylorism', that, although used in many organizations, no longer meets the present requirements;
• creating organizational architectures focussed on durability and coherence.

SqEME® approaches these issues with the help of four windows. The desire to look at organizations by means of the four windows originates through the monitoring of organizations that has developed during the twentieth century. This development, as we briefly describe it, can be found in chapter 1. Chapter 2 describes the four windows, Constitution, Chemistry, Correspondence and Construction. The use of these windows is an important starting point in terms of the SqEME® methodology; a way of how one should look at an enterprise. For the connoisseur, this view can be compared to the tradition of phenomenology. As in phenomenology, SqEME® starts with the direct and intuitive experience of discovering the essential qualities of processes. Just as in the phenomenological tradition, SqEME® dissociates itself from the alienation and the denial of the human being in the organization and regards this human (the professional) as the primary source of energy and information. These central themes of SqEME® are also covered in chapter 2.

In chapter 3 this methodology will be converted into a practical method. SqEME® Process Management constitutes a consistent and coherent set of modelling techniques, the so-called 'language and signs'. These are described in chapter 3 and worked through in detail in chapters 4 to 7. The four chapters Constitution, Chemistry, Correspondence and Construction form the heart of this book. They are the essential practical stages and form the ontology for the development towards a process driven organization.

Chapter 4 focuses at the Architecture of the enterprise by looking at the Key Result Areas. The chapter is about process thinking and focuses upon the principles and values that lie behind this, translated in the modelling of Key Result Areas that should be a particular point of attention for senior managers. Chapter 5 is about communication between people in the organization. Thinking in process terms refers to the flow of energy in organization, patterns in communication and influence. SqEME® uses the term 'chemistry' in the organization. It is especially of interest to people involved with semantics, communication and information flows. Chapter 6, Construction, covers the process thinking aimed at the architecture of the organization, the deployment of tasks to people, the provisioning and use of resources and the implementation of procedures. In relation to this, particular attention should be paid to the types of roles in an organization, the allocation of authority amongst them and the relationships between tasks, responsibilities and authority.

Chapter 7 explains how the Correspondence window can be used to monitor how the organization is performing. The focus is on ensuring that business processes are being executed as planned and that their performance is matching the objectives that have been set of them.

Following earlier references, chapter 8 investigates how an organization might handle the requirements of process accountability, and who in the organization might be responsible for the quality of processes.

Thereafter, in chapter 9 we investigate the potential use of the SqEME® approach to address organizational and managerial issues. Finally, in Chapter 10 we revisit some of the key issues in implementing the method successfully on a step-by-step basis and examine how supporting software can be utilised when applying SqEME®.

1   Developments

Over time many ideas and applications of process management have arisen. The SqEME® method is a contemporary interpretation of managing processes. A translation of how we want to organize work these days, based upon the current context and preconditions. In this chapter, a number of developments that form the basis of this translation will be drawn from the Organization Theory. We will also take a look at the likely implications of current information technology upon the design of our organizations, together with how this may affect the way we handle processes.

1.1   The Inheritance of One Hundred Years of Functional School

Process management certainly is not a new theme. Over a period of time, lots of different approaches of process management have been developed and applied. Standardizing production through working with conveyor belts in the days of Taylor and Ford at the start of the previous century could be regarded as a form of process management. Hardjono and Bakker[1] describe this approach to process management as scientific management, an approach of the Functional School. Significantly, this approach seeks to describe and define processes in such a way that these processes can be split up into the smallest possible tasks in order to achieve more efficiency by short learning cycles and a minimum of time spent on them. Hardjono and Bakker indicate that this definition is contradictory to the view of processes as a sequence of single events defined by time and motion, a view that better matches the SqEME® approach.

Scientific management can truly be called the most dominant paradigm of the twentieth century. This is particularly the case in American (or Anglo-Saxon) management theory, where the principles of scientific management have assumed an important position.

The application of the principles of standardization, specialization, maximization, concentration, centralization and synchronization has resulted in an unprecedented increase in efficiency, and when combined with market opportunities, also in wealth[2]. On the other hand, the main drawback of scientific management (and the functional school as a whole) is not the perspective itself. This is valuable and still makes an important contribution to the performance of organizations. However, the principles are so rooted in our managerial thinking, that they pose the question of whether we are actually able to organize in another manner[3]. It seems as though we have been caught by it, preventing us from exploiting technological possibilities, especially when we also want to take into account the social reality of the twenty-first century.

In the first half of the twentieth century these principles were a major influence, particularly in car factories, textile and clothing factories and the food processing industry, in other words the

---

[1] Hardjono and Bakker (2006), Management of Processes.
[2] Toffler (1980), The Third wave.
[3] Morgan (1986), Images Of Organization, p. 6

mechanized production process[4]. They later found their way to other parts of the organization (e.g. administrative processes) and to organizations that had no production processes whatsoever, such as in the service sector and in the public sector (e.g. banks, insurance companies and executive departments of the governmental organizations). Morgan indicates that the application of scientific management in these types of organizations has lead to a sort of 'office factories'. In an environment like that, one is expected to work certain regular hours and perform pre-determined activities. Employees have become specialists in certain tasks and are monitored thoroughly in relation to errors and time performance. In numerous departments claims are settled, insurances are taken out, contracts are reviewed, allowances are paid, subsidies are granted, and clerical work is done in this way[5]. In this approach, Process Management seems to adhere to the presupposition of controllability and predictability from a technical system perspective. The main characteristics of scientific management are that the planning and design of work are strictly separated from its execution. There is separation between 'thinking' and 'doing'. The managers have the overview and design the work from that perspective. Just as with a machine, the point is to have a rational knowledge of what is going on inside the organization.

Management has to model the organization along the lines of a predictable machine. These models supply management with the feeling of control, of controllability. The (working) human being is not the primary source of information but rather the weakest link in the system.

Arising out of scientific management, a dominant way of organizing has developed, strikingly described by Morgan in his book 'Images of Organization'. This approach to organizing has been given the name 'machine bureaucracy' by the German sociologist Weber. Weber studied the mechanization of the industry and subsequently drew the parallel with the development of bureaucratic forms of organizing. Next to precisely defined tasks there are precisely defined lines of accountability and information supply. In these, so called, staff-line-organizations, employees get their information via the vertical hierarchy. Reports are sent upwards and assignments are sent down. Although Weber is the intellectual father of the term machine bureaucracy, this does not mean that he would be a great supporter of this type of organizing. On the contrary, Weber himself stated that despite the large potential of the bureaucratic approach, the inspiration and spontaneity of people would be subject to erosion because every aspect of human action would become mechanical and routine[6].

It is worth noting that Taylor's book was translated into Russian in 1912 and that one of the readers was Lenin. In addition, the centrally controlled communist economy as designed by Lenin -and of which we know the conclusion by now- has all the characteristics of the machine bureaucracy.

When one recognizes that the present society in essence is dominated by this type of organizing, one can easily guess where the reaction of interest for spirituality, creativity and deepening finds its origin. We have built giant 'learning factories', whilst nursing homes and hospitals grow ever larger and become more 'human-denying'. Companies and governmental organizations merge under the guise of advantages of scale. Larger is better, because it is more efficient.

---

4   Womack, Jones and Roos (1990), The Machine That Changed The World.
5   Morgan (1986), Images of Organization, p. 24
6   Morgan (1986), Images of Organization, p. 17

When the problem gets large enough –and grows out of the organizational boundaries- yet larger organizations have to be created, in order to have the hierarchical structure to bear the responsibility for its solution. In this way, the public transport problem in the urban sprawl in the western part of the Netherlands should be solved by simply merging all local public transport companies in the area. Safety, a problem that has consequences for several ministries, could be solved by the creation of one 'super-ministry'.

The inability to cooperate at an administrative level could be solved by means of a super-province. In this perspective, the introduction of programme and project management in governmental organizations seems to be a good counterweight.

A countermovement is the search for organization forms that are of a smaller scale, more human and more durable. At scale enlargement we can increasingly difficult foresee what the effect of an intervention will be. It becomes so complex that you can't predict what at the end the effect or the return on the investment will be. Also, scale enlargement anonimizes and can lead to the forming of 'private kingdoms' and to indifference. Departments do not work together and sometimes even fight each other. Top management is not always in control of the ongoing business and is frequently surprised by new or changing circumstances in their own organization. In an environment such as that, plans and objectives have to stand by themselves. Employees will be decreasingly inclined to take the responsibility for their own actions. Instead, they will strive for their own interest rather than support the objectives of the organization. All these factors make managers feel the need for more bureaucratic control, resulting in a self-centred syrupy organization. Management structures will be created that can only be described as giant, ponderous, top-down and mechanical. The distance between management, (the decisions) and the work floor (the reality) will only grow in this way. Expressed in metaphoric terms, we are building 'towers of Babel'. Another characteristic of the tower of Babel was that it drew building materials (energy) from its surroundings without developing these itself. It became a system, sponging upon its environment, at best maintaining itself, without supplying any extra value –at least not to its surroundings-. Relate this to the discussion about durability and shortage. Where organizations lose contact with their environment, they lose their reason for existence, their 'licence to operate'.

In a rapidly changing environment, this type of organization will have a very hard time. Such organizations run the risk that process management unintentionally leads to even greater bureaucracy and fossilization: the development of fully documented flowcharts in heavy procedural handbooks. The SqEME® approach to process management aims at turning the tide by asking for attention to processes and process management in another manner.

1.2   The Transition to an Information Society

In his book 'Powershift', Toffler describes the autonomous employee. With the principle of the autonomous employee, he exposes the social discontinuity between the age of industrialization (with, as a guideline, machine technology) and the social order of the present period (with information technology as a guideline) that we are currently discovering. Based upon his own experiences as an employee on an assembly line, he describes his vision of the future of the employee in the information era.

The most important conclusion is that anywhere where new technologies are available, new ways of working have to appear in order to utilize them.

As a new way of working, namely scientific management, came into existence through the development of the machine, the conveyor belt and the factory, this will also happen as a result of information and communication technology. Toffler describes how scientific management blossomed because at the time of the rise of the factories one was dealing with an agricultural society. Labourers were not skilled and they were used to working in a family environment. Working in a factory required a new structure and a new way of supervising. Work had to be divided in small standardized activities that were easy to learn and made employees replaceable[7]. Toffler goes on to illustrate that if the old agricultural way of working had been continued whilst working on assembly lines, then the use of machine technology would never have grown and the giant increases of efficiency would never have been achieved. Genuinely new technologies like ICT also require a new way of working. The biggest mistake we can make, according to Toffler, is to leave the advantages of ICT unused, by refusing to change the principles of the existing way of working. It is painful to notice that in many cases ICT has also become the prisoner of bureaucratic thinking. It requires a completely different approach to enable a breakthrough, or at least the start of a transition.

An emphasis on looking at information and the interaction aspects of an organization and their resultant impact upon processes could contribute to a new way of thinking. This new way of thinking is –among others- pointed out by Friedman. In his book 'The World is Flat' he describes how organizations are confronted by the development that all routine activities are taken out of their hands through the arrival of ICT. Either through computer automation itself, or by outsourcing these activities to other countries where workers with an appropriate education perform the same tasks at a lower cost. Do not just think of the answering of phone calls and the processing of tax forms, but also the handling of complete administrative procedures and processes. There is a shift towards activities that are not routine or – to put it in a better way- less predictable. Work that has to do with (market) leadership, inter-human relationship and creativity[8]. The most important starting point of the Taylorian thinking, namely the idea that human actions should be reduced and standardized so that people and their operations are made into (exchangeable) shackles in a supply chain, has been left in the points of view of Friedman and others. Partially as a result of this, one should not regard employees as replaceable 'resources'. Professionals should be seen as the capital, the essentials and the potential of the enterprise. In other words, in the industrial period employees were small cogwheels in the machine, performing standardized routine activities. In the information society, the whole system of creation of value is designed around the professional maturity of the employees. When an employee leaves the organization, he takes a wealth of implicit knowledge with him, along with his contacts and networks. Metaphorically speaking, employees are not the production factors, but rather they actually own the production factors in the form of knowledge and relations.

---

[7]   Toffler (1990), Powershift, chapter 18
[8]   Friedman (2006), The World is Flat, p. 15.

For the creation of additional value, as Toffler describes, we increasingly have to deal with growing amounts of information and communication that have to be processed.

In the machine bureaucracy, the processing of information is the domain of specialist (staff) senior Management in the vertical hierarchy. Enabled by the growing possibilities of ICT, employees can gain an appreciation of operational management as a whole and, from there, to think about their contribution to it. This stands or falls with the willingness of all members of the organization to share information. Improving the organization by aiming for a better 'information position' of the individual employee on the one hand offers new possibilities, whilst on the other hand it forms a threat to the current 'power elite'. In the past management or staff derived their position from the fact that they had a better overall view of information than others. The new form of organization starts from the point of trust in the self-control of employees. This is a development towards the reunification of thinking and acting, where everyone is manager of their own job. The authority to make decisions is redistributed and from a management perspective this means that the vertical structures in the organization, the hierarchy, get another meaning[9].

In other words, just as during the twentieth century when machine bureaucracy, the dominant organization form, originated from scientific management, so in the information era a new dominant form of cooperation will evolve, with more emphasis upon the horizontal relations. Organizations will be more focused on humans and the qualities they can utilise. At the same time, organizing will be on a smaller scale. It will focus on the smallest possible principle of organizing: the client-supplier relationship, for example the relationship between professional and customer, or the one between employees transferring information and results to each other. The meaning of 'small scale' will be different than it was during the twentieth century. Organizing will be the connecting of unique variables that together will form powerful (network-like) structures, of which the boundaries are undetermined and more or less invisible. This will be powerful enough to become an alternative for the large organizations of the twentieth century, but with a completely unique form of complexity. Organizations are more likely to be inclined to operate in temporary cooperative structures in order to achieve results. Smaller scale organizational units with less (though better equipped and more dedicated) employees, that work together with others in an efficient and effective way. Gradually a whole jumble (conglomeration) of cooperative relationships will appear which will alter depending on the subject. Because the cooperative themes are usually connected to people, we are likely to talk about value chains and networks when we discuss this phenomenon. It becomes increasingly difficult to talk about organizations and to distinguish organization structures. The focus shifts from organizations to organizing.

From the perspective of process management it is interesting to look at how we can contribute to this development. The execution of processes is vulnerable and strongly depends on good information supply. The SqEME® approach to processes requires detailed attention to the communication between processes. It is important to invest in the quality of the communication between the employees. In this sense, the quality of the process and the information supply are two sides of the same coin.

---

[9]   Toffler (1990), Powershift, chapter 18

1.3   Developments in ICT and Organizations

Another important approach to processes has been in the shape of Business Process Reengineering (BPR), described, amongst others, by Hammer and Champy and by Davenport. Just as with the quality movement, they urged managers to fundamentally change their view of the working methods in their organization. Operational processes had to be revised and completely reconsidered[10]. By fundamentally redesigning the operational processes, the organization could achieve significant improvements in its performance[11]. BPR has been welcomed by many companies, especially in America, but also in other Anglo-Saxon countries. Unfortunately, the approach has been (mis)used for the rigorous reduction (sometimes by more than 20%) of operational staff[12]. This was within the bureaucratic tradition for which BPR had, in fact, become an alternative. After all, the intention was to redesign the organization of the traditional machine bureaucracy. Perhaps because of this, a large amount of criticism was generated against BPM: the approach would be founded upon a technical system perspective, it would just be scientific management in disguise. Apart from this, the criticism focused on the approach to change that has been used in combination with this method. Hammer himself indicates that one of the most important plusses of BPR has been that 'reengineering' has changed the perspective of top managers. Supervisors no longer see their organization as a set of separate units that are strictly separated by precisely defined borders. Supervisors have learned to perceive the organization as a whole, incorporating flexible groups that are undertaking interwoven activities and information exchange, cutting through the organization horizontally, and ending at the points where the contact with clients takes place[13]. Thus, it remains interesting to study the principles behind BPR in more detail. For this we refer to the work of Hammer (1990), Hammer and Champy (1993), Davenport (1990 and 1993) and Hammer and Stanton (1999).

In spite of the appeal of BPR to change the view at the organization, it did not offer any tools or techniques to do this. In addition, the approach was not able to refer back to a long history. A second chance for BPR came by way of a different approach to process management, namely that of Business Process Management (BPM). BPM differs from BPR because it uses a more incremental approach (just like SqEME®) rather than redesigning the organization in a radical way. Above all, BPM puts the opportunities for new technological developments at the centre of focus[attention]. The attraction of looking at organizations in a different way coincides with the opportunities offered by ICT. This approach to process management is, amongst others, described by Smith and Fingar in their book 'Business Process Management, the third wave'. Whereas Toffler, in a book titled partially the same, gave his vision on the rise of the 'information society'[14], Smith and Fingar describe a method that should enable organizations to meet the demands of the information society and to exploit its opportunities[15]. Thus, BPM is presented as a completely new approach, in the sense that an entirely new key concept is introduced. Where in BPR 'efficiency' was principally placed at the centre, in particular the rationalization and optimisation of the processes that were to be automated, the central theme of BPM is 'agility',

---

[10] Hammer (1990), Reengineering Work: Don't automate, obliterate, p. 104-112
[11] Hammer and Champy (1993), Reengineering the Corporation: A Manifesto for Business Revolution
[12] Internet: http://en.wikipedia.org/wiki/Business_process_reengineering (feb. 2007).
[13] Hammer and Stanton (1999), How Process Enterprises Really Work
[14] Toffler (1980), The Third wave
[15] Smith and Fingar (2003), Business Process Management, the third wave

meaning something like 'flexibility'. This 'agility' approach is of great importance. Nevertheless, it is a fact that the ICT world is still ruled by a form of 'engineers' thinking'. This thinking strongly resembles the machine bureaucratic ideas. If we think of the statement by Einstein that problems cannot be solved at the level at which they occurred, then an impulse should come from the outside in order to fully realise the potential benefits of the 'agility' approach. Such an impulse can only come from the 'demanding side'; accountable management. It should come up with a thoroughly worked out plan about the framework (i.e. architecture) of the organization.

The traditional ICT approach to process management is focused strongly upon the automation of workflows (Workflow Management). In their book 'Service Orient or be Doomed' Bloomberg and Schmelzer explain that the problem of contemporary 'workflow' automation is that the developers of systems such as this want to control the organization far too much. The idea is that the processes, once documented, will always be the processes as we want to use them. However, 'agility' implies the ability to move continuously, in response to the changes in the environment. ICT now tries to get a closer connection to 'business'. ICT should be organized in such a way that it enables processes which match the strategy of the organization in the ever-changing environment. Changes should be made step-by-step. 'Agile' organizations are organizations that consider changes as a way of continuously improving their own organization[16]. At this moment, lots of attention is generated for principles like Service-Oriented Architecture, XML, ESB and web services that, combined with new ways of working, really can give meaning to the concept of 'agility'. All of this, still under the name 'Enterprise Architecture', suggests that the concept of stand-alone organizational units still exists.

The relation between the contemporary process approach as we have modelled with SqEME® and the process approach to ICT is based upon a love-hate relationship. In fact, a severe tension exists. Views of process management originating from ICT can almost always be interpreted as the technical system perspective. A characteristic to this perspective is that there is no difference between system acts and human acts. This means that organizations that architect their processes according to the principles of the functional school or Taylorism, get stuck with processes that metaphorically resemble the Charlie Chaplin-like situations known from the film 'Modern Times', in which employees perform actions that are determined by the routine of technology. Bloomberg and Schmelzer criticize this work arising out of the technical system perspective and emphasize that we should ensure that the technology supports the work routines of the employees. This is an idea that matches the SqEME® approach.

As pointed out by the EFQM Excellence Model, it is not appropriate to describe employees as 'resources' that we can employ in previously developed workflows. On the contrary, the authors say, the automated workflows should be seen as 'resources' and be at the service of the employees themselves[17]. It is Fingar, the second author of 'Business Process Management, the third wave', who predicted a fourth wave, i.e. the 'human interactive processes'[18]. In this (in fact remarkable) stage, the developments in ICT come together with the developments in the area of organization and quality sciences. Where the world of information technology revalues the human-human

---

[16] Bloomberg and Schmelzer (2006), Service orient or be doomed, p. 12
[17] Bloomberg and Schmelzer (2006), Service orient or be doomed, p. 57-59.
[18] Internet http://www.human-interaction-management.info (Feb. 2007).

processes, organization science and, in particular, the quality tradition has had this perspective as a starting point since the 1960s. We do not mean methods like SPC and Six Sigma, but rather the Open System Thinking of Bertalanffy, Katz and Kahn, and Emery and Trist, and the quality thinking Juran, Deming and Weick, amongst others. In these traditions, people are not the 'resources' of the organization; instead, in essence, organizations exist because of (and through the support of) people. We call this the social system perspective. We should also point out that some authors see the series 'closed system – open system – social system' as degrees of complexity in the thinking about organizations.

An important development in recent years has been the 'meeting of minds' of the technical system perspective and this social system perspective in the process orientation. In this, the social system perspective is not an extension of the technical system perspective. It is a completely different view of the operation of organizations. The social system perspective is based upon the scientific approach of the phenomenology and the 'social constructivism' in which there is –as a result- a great deal of attention paid to the stories employees have to tell and the way they experience situations. At the point at which these perspectives merge, inherently semantic discussions appear. The concept of what a 'process' is can differ from person to person. Also, the members of an organization will approach the information supply or the employment of ICT in a completely different manner. The differences in the perception of the organization lead to different interpretation of data, to different information flows and different utilization of IT solutions. The information that people in an organization give each other is often more based on what they THINK their colleagues need, then on clear agreements. That phenomenon effect also the use of IT. Illustrative of this development are statements from suppliers of ICT and BPM solutions, like 'we should learn to speak the language of business'. In other words, they should learn to understand the stories of employees. As an approach, the technical system perspective and the social system perspective do absolutely not exclude each other. In practice, both perspectives prove to be equally valid and can co-exist. They manifest themselves in much the same way as the metaphorical 'old woman and young lady', the picture that can be perceived both as an old woman and as a young lady, but only as one of them at a time, never in both ways at the same moment. People perceiving the old woman might describe what they see; however, whilst they are describing the same picture, they actually mention different characteristics than those that somebody describing the young lady might see. This metaphor clearly indicates, as described by Covey, how strongly conditioned our perception is (as with our paradigms). In the longer term, our behaviour (so also our organization forms) is not effective if we are not completely conscious of our basic paradigms[19].

The central starting point of the social system perspective is that it is the people in the organization that have the power and can use their power to enable the organization to excel. De facto, they are the organization. The people have the power to respond to new circumstances, the power to find new solutions and the power to step out of the traditional mental frameworks. The most important power they have is the so-called power to socialize: the ability to work together with others. The other powers are the materials, the commercial power and the intellectual power[20]. These powers stretch a little beyond what the term 'agility' suggests at first glance. In order to

---

[19] Covey (1989), The seven habits of highly effective people, p. 20
[20] Hardjono (1997), (Rythm and Organizational Dynamics) *Ritmiek en organisatiedynamiek*

address these we are dependent upon the knowledge, the skills and the effort of all employees in the organization. Creating value is not just about the transformation of raw materials into products or the supply of standard services. It is not just the hands that are important, the creation of value is in the head and in the heart. This means that successful and sustainable organizations are, from the social system perspective, able to address the potential of people.

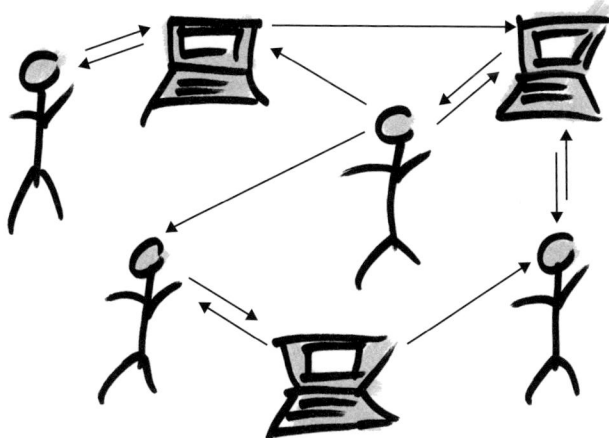

Figure 1.1   Technical system perspective or social system perspective? Focus on technology or focus on human being?

Process management from this perspective is about investing in coherence, about cooperation and about providing an insight into how the activities and expertise of employees contribute to the whole. A social system perspective like this provides a completely different approach to the developments in ICT. From this perspective, ICT is synonymous with connecting people. ICT enables the sharing of information between people and, by doing this, enables them to unite. Information as a concept has a social meaning. People have to be aware of the relevance of information for others and be willing to share meaningful information and to distribute it. On the other hand, people should also be aware of the relevance of information in relation to their work and be willing to receive information and to really do something with it. In this respect, along with the developments in ICT, the importance of a social system perspective is growing.

The 'world of ICT' (the technical system perspective) and the 'quality tradition'
(the social system perspective) come together in the growing importance of information in organizations: the connecting of people'. The SqEME® approach aims at serving both types of interests, and complies with the needs of both by respecting the human processes as well as the ICT processes that relate to information supply.

1.4   Out of Control

The emergence of 'flexibility' and 'creativity' as orientations for the organizing of processes makes it necessary to deepen the perspective of control. As described earlier, the need for control strongly determines our present way of organizing and our way to change. Most of our management thinking is based upon getting the organization under control. In some situations, for example in some public institutions like the Police and the Public Prosecution Office, but also in fast developing markets such as communication and consumer electronics, the predictability of developments is limited. The threats likely to be posed in two years time is hard to predict, and the developments in the communication industry are so fast that many of us have just a vague picture of the market in five years. This requires another perception of 'control'. Not based upon predictability, but one that transcends technology. A form of control of technology in the sense that one can discuss the situation with the help of technology without being dominated by it, so to speak to be 'liberated' from it. In his book 'Out of Control', Kelly describes a number of principles that are applicable in a context like this. Also for the management of processes these principles have an important meaning[21]:

- A way of working does not have to be studied, thought over, understood and planned in advance. Processes arise and develop themselves continuously. Every time we carry out a task, either in cooperation or not, we learn from its execution. This continuously improves operational procedures. Successful solutions reinforce themselves, and in turn produce successful solutions again. This creates patterns of working. Also De Bono describes this phenomenon in his book 'Mechanism of Mind'[22].
- New complex organizational solutions cannot be implemented at once or rolled out at once. It is better to start small with parts that work. From there, one can build on to the more complex solution.

The development of complex solutions just takes time. Even when all parts are present, time is necessary in order to test each part in interaction with the other. When one studies different parts in their relation, complexity exists by definition. Seen through today's eyes, the first motor cars are extremely primitive machines. Still, you could drive them and sometimes even drive them fast. Modern cars are complex systems, as a result of one hundred twenty-five years of development, systems that the designers could never have predicted.

Uniformity of working may seem efficient, but this advantage disappears when the circumstances change. At that stage, major changes in the organization are necessary. Besides universality, organizations in a changing environment need a certain degree of diversity. Allowing diversity (in the way of working) stimulates adaptations and changes in the organization. These changes do not manifest themselves as a few large leaps, but instead proceed gradually, in thousands of small steps. In such organizations, according to amongst others Zuijderhoudt and Stacey, germs of ideas can grow that, through discontinuity, lead to innovation. This idea is also a fundamental point of Kaizen, the key to Japanese competitive success[23].

Changes are inherently and always accompanied by 'errors' that are made in respect to written plans and procedures. In changing organizations, these 'errors' appear. Incrementally improving the organization can in this respect be seen as a systematic way of 'error' management. At the moment that defects become apparent, it is important how to respond to them. In this respect, the importance of learning from errors is greater than preventing them. 'Errors' are not the

---

[21] Kelly (1994), Out of Control, p. 468-470
[22] De Bono (1969), Mechanism of Mind, p. 61-65
[23] Imai (1990), Kaizen – The Key to Japan's Competitive Success

basis to judge and punish others, but to learn from as a collective. This can be practiced both in predictable surroundings and in those environments where processes with unpredictable results take place. Under all circumstances, management should have the guts to admit that a chosen way has been wrong, instead of staying on this course against one's better judgement. You should accept your loss and try another way of working. Only by doing this, can the thousands of minute changes be made that enable the organization to continuously create value. In an environment full of predictable processes, something like a Six Sigma programme is possible. A Six Sigma programme is, in essence, more concerned with a company's investment in increasing its learning abilities, rather than explicitly enlarging the control of processes. It urges the people in the organization to investigate every error or unforeseen circumstance in detail, especially because it is hard to believe that the occurrence of these circumstances might have been caused just by coincidence. In this respect one should keep in mind that the 'dispersion', the number of sigma's, is determined by the process and not by management.

Only machines can be optimally predictable in their execution. Organizations are not machines and can, therefore, more easily agree on acceptable ways of working for a period of time, knowing that they are capable of evolving continuously. When it works, it is good enough! Besides, organizations can, in contrast with machines, strive for more than one goal and follow several paths at the same time. Optimising operations for one goal might harm other interests. In this respect, accepting 'out of control' and trusting upon the self-organizing abilities present in an organization have more in common, than it seems at first glance, with our dominant 'control-driven' attitude!

2 Methodology

The design of the operational management, the process approach, the assignment of roles, how this is dealt with and way in which this is managed, all these aspects form a complex matter. It is and will be the work of humans; people are at the heart of organizing the work. Primarily, organizational development is about the influencing the behaviour of the collective of individuals in a certain desirable direction. From the SqEME® method, the organization is seen as a social system. Human beings are at the heart of it. According to Weick, it is a characteristic of process thinking that man is the defining factor; it is not the organizational structure that should be the object of process management but rather the interactive process that takes place between humans,[24]. As Weick puts it, it might be better to talk about 'organizing' than about 'organizations'. The basic principle behind the SqEME® method is that an organization is essentially a bundling of processes, put into effect by inspired professionals. These professionals arrive at results on the basis of their craftsmanship, effective information services and practical tools.

2.1 Mental Model

The social system perspective of the SqEME® method requires another approach rather than the current deterministic approach. Therefore, the mental model behind the SqEME® method has a more holistic foundation. The word 'holistic' can be defined as 'based on a theory (originally set up for biology) to explain 'life', in which the entirety, the mutual connection and the cooperation of the parts are key issues'. The SqEME® method claims that organizations should be seen from their totality as much as possible: the organization as an alliance of people.

The total view is studied via the SqEME® method by posing four basic questions: What are the essential building blocks of the enterprise? What is the bond that unites the professionals? How is the execution of the work organized? How do we perform in undertaking our business?

The thinking model that forms the basis of the SqEME® method is visualized by means of four windows. These four windows are called Constitution, Chemistry, Construction and Correspondence. Each one of them enables its own view and has its own 'colour' and its own shape. These windows do not form a 2 by 2 matrix in which the windows can be put side by side in relation to two axes. Each window tells its own specific story and can not be separated from the (holistic) whole. Through the use of the four windows, a coherent view will be created and a deeper insight gained into the organization as a whole. With one eye it is difficult to see depth. The four windows are complementary and lead to a consistent, specific and verifiable understanding of reality.

The Constitution window asks people in an organization to take a look at 'the other side of the picture' by formulating the management philosophy: what is the idea behind the existence of the organization? What are the moral and ideological starting points? What are the value

---

[24] Weick (1979), The social psychology of organizing; Hardjono and Bakker (2006), *Management van processen.*

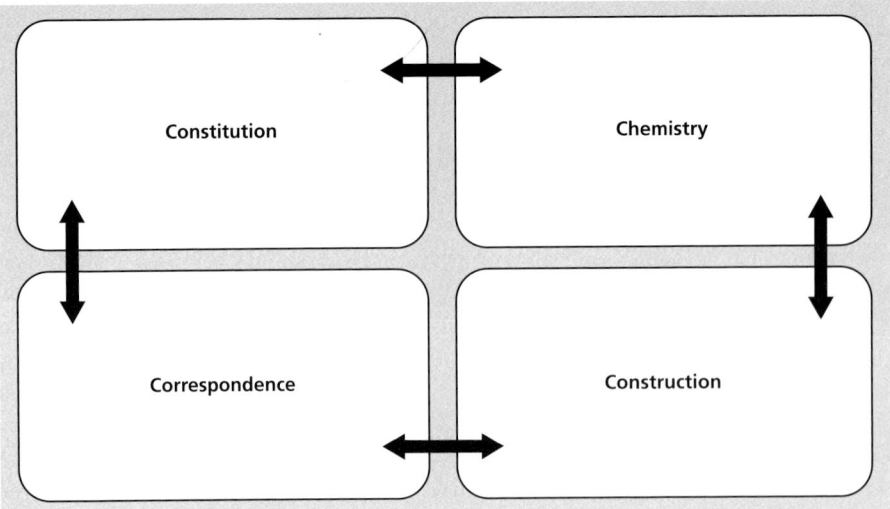

Figure 2.1   The four windows of the SqEME®methodology

systems of the individuals within the organization and what is the preferred value system within the enterprise? How are they translated into a vision, followed by a mission and a strategy for the organization? Constitution stands for the basic ideas, the ethics, for the basic characteristics of the enterprise. Constitution also stands for aesthetics: what makes someone perceive the organization as 'beautiful'? This constitution is what you 'taste' when you physically enter the organization, or even when talking with an employee over the phone. They are the basic patterns that are present in everything that is being done in the organization. Constitution is the DNA of the organization.

Through the Chemistry window people in an organization can get a view at what initiates and keeps the organization in motion: the spirit of cooperation between people. The interaction between people, both inside and outside the organization, is studied through the Chemistry window. This window provides an insight in the 'game of forces' between the interests and the interested. Where there is no tension there is no life! It is about leadership, about inspiration, enthusiasm and passion. Where is the energy, what does it mean to you? What makes this organization work? Chemistry stands for the organization as a transformation process, for the interaction between people. Chemistry also stands for the relationship of the organization with the environment. From the perspective of open system thinking this means that the organization is in continuous exchange with its surrounding and that this provides the organization with its 'license to operate'. The social system thinking even goes one step further: attention for the real interaction, the mutual added value and the interdependence.

In the Construction window the tangible reality appears, how things manifest themselves in reality. This window is the most visible and most tangible one. How is the operation designed? Within organizations, this means the employment of people and means. It is about the people, the materials, the budgets, about supplying laptops, company cars and ICT facilities. All the resources that are necessary to enable operation. Construction is also about the employment of people. It is about the distribution of tasks, responsibilities and power. Who reports to whom? It also covers the employment of expertise, the supply of information, the design of training and the facilitation of craftsmanship. Construction embodies the organization in its real appearance.

Finally, the Correspondence window provides a view at how the organization actually operates. The dynamics of the organization are studied and monitored. Among the followers of 'to measure is to know' this window is very popular. It is about the monitoring and 'getting in control' of the organization. How does the organization perform? What are the targets? It is the window that covers management data, reports, future analyses and benchmarking. Starting from the principle of 'out of control', this window is about continuous education, recognizing patterns, agreement upon the framing, the bandwidths for self-organizing enterprises. Instruments like the Business Balanced Scorecard and management information systems appear in this window. It is the window of operational research, of statistics, but also of gut feelings. The reality is to be visualized, measured and discussed objectively or at least inter-subjectively. Inter-subjectivity is a very important term within the SqEME® approach. On the matter of understanding organizations objectivity does not exist. What does exist is an inter-subjective truth. When most people see it that way, than that is the truth. So a shared picture of the processes of the enterprise is not an objective fact but an inter-subjective truth.

Through this window, one investigates whether things go as they are planned, expected or desired. From the description that is derived, initiatives can put in place to take action with respect to the Constitution, Chemistry or Construction of the organization.

2.2 Principles

The principles that are the basis of the SqEME® method have become clearer over the years. Essentially they form the 'lessons learned' in terms of the developments in the last decades around the management of processes. In chapter one of this book we went into the matter of these developments. The following four leading principles are representative of the way in which the SqEME® method handles these developments:
1. Result-oriented management in the context of inclusive thinking and open system thinking.
2. Information supply as an incentive for 'horizontal organizing'.
3. Building blocks and patterns for the structuring of processes.
4. The professionally mature employee as a starting point.

Result-oriented management in the context of inclusive thinking and open system thinking
SqEME® for process management uses the term *inclusive thinking*. The term *inclusive thinking* has been adopted from the philosopher Feitse Boerwinkel. It introduces an alternative to antagonistic thinking (thinking in contrasts) and exclusive, egocentric thinking. He describes it as: 'A thinking that is fundamentally based upon the idea that my good (luck, life, welfare) is not achieved at the cost of or without the other, but that it can only be obtained if that person at the same time intends to achieve and improve the good of the other.'[25] The fundamental point of inclusive thinking is the consciousness that humanity forms one family and that one cannot harm the fellow human without -in him- injuring oneself. Or, expressed more positively, the consciousness that one only achieves full development if one does not focus solely upon oneself

---

[25] Boerwinkel 1966

but cooperates extensively with others. As Boerwinkel states, 'man is no longer worth what their own brain is worth, but what all the brains of all people are worth'. He argues for the need to abandon antagonistic and exclusive thinking, stating that any war will in the end only have losers and that Europe, after many hundreds of years of warfare, has finally discovered that cooperation is ultimately more profitable. Apart from this, numerous evidence has been gathered and dozens of exercises have illustrated that cooperation leads to improved results compared with going your own way.

Inclusive thinking propagates a ban on the making of enemy images, as well as ways of thinking that are derived from warfare. Inclusive thinking stands for empathizing with the ways of thinking of others. This attitude is necessary to abandon 'departmental thinking' in favour of a way of thinking in which people take responsibility for each other's acts and ultimately for the common results. Stated in simple terms, it is a remedy for 'internal political games' and contributes to a culture in which people assume their responsibilities in the knowledge that their interest is dependent upon the common interest. In this way, it is also an approach to express the ideas of Weick. Only when you try to really understand the thoughts and ideas of others, will you succeed in conquering and preventing ambiguities in communication.

With this philosophical approach, SqEME® underlines that it is not only sensible, but also necessary to get to the truth of the basic principles, the philosophical fundaments, the possible religious roots and the cultural characteristics of an enterprise. To achieve this, SqEME® uses the concepts of *Constitution*. For SqEME® as a method, the essential starting point is inclusive thinking, including the following guidelines that Boerwinkel supplies for inclusive thinking:
- One has to beware of considering oneself superior to others and one has to avoid 'self-righteousness'.
- One has to assume the other is convinced in his opinions.
- One has to be willing to listen to the other and be aware of one's own beliefs.
- One has to beware of stereotyping.
- One has to find a solution to both work and live together by helping and encouraging each other and, where required, providing clear criticism and, if absolutely necessary, opposition.

The choice for inclusive thinking is not meant to be idealistic in the first place. SqEME® shares the opinion of Boerwinkel that it is a realistic choice. Process management is not meant to present things in a better light than they actually are. SqEME® Process Management is mainly intended to make the organization result-oriented , and results that are achieved at the expense of others will only lead in short term to opposition, or in the longer term to rebellion or forceful counteraction. Just keeping in mind one's own self-interest is not only proof of short term thinking, but is also foolish as it focuses upon immediate results without any long term considerations. Process management is also about cooperation and, from this perspective, the concept of inclusive thinking is a powerful and meaningful starting point. The necessity to cooperate with others finds its origin in the idea that organizations are open systems. On this subject, SqEME® embraces the notions of Senge and the ideas of Emery and Trist ('managing the boundary conditions').

Information supply as an incentive for horizontal organizing

The shift in the traditional concept of process thinking is described in literature as the shift from a vertical approach of an organization to a horizontal approach. This implies something else than the 'tilting of an organization'. With the tilting of the organization, the traditional principles of thinking in terms of tasks and responsibilities and the institution of a hierarchy that has to supervise their correct implementation are in fact maintained. The supplementary effect of holding on to this way of thinking is that one opts for a matrix organization in which employees get two superiors: a functional and an operational boss, introducing various conflicts of interest and the opportunity to play off one boss against the other. Matrix organizations work beautifully on paper but appear to function only rarely in practice. Yet, organizations wishing to change over to process-driven operations seem to choose intermediate solution like this and appoint so-called process managers who sometimes get a functional task or sometimes an operational one. Often this leads to the effect that line management or the employees come to stand opposite to the process-managers. The energy is not bundled, instead the company has created a loss or leakage of energy.

SqEME® Process Management takes the view that an organization should be considered as a bundling of processes[26] in which the main subject is internal communication; the organization can therefore be viewed as an 'information processing system'. From this point of view, on one the hand one discovers imperfections and barriers that explain why up till now things have never gone as they were expected to. On the other hand one, only then sees what has to be done to really make new technologies work; in fact to make an organization into an integral system, in which employees only have to respond to exceptional situations, because automated production and control systems adequately respond to all standard situations. Reacting to exceptional situations after all means freedom of action, in which the essence is to make choices that match the objectives of the organization, with less emphasis placed upon the way in which they are achieved. In fact SqEME® adopts the idea that functional/hierarchical organizing and Taylorism and Scientific Management have passed their expiry date. SqEME® particularly focuses upon the information/communication processes and on the correctness and completeness of this information. Just as in a Kanban-system[27], an empty basket is the signal to start producing. No more but also no less than is necessary to fill up the basket again. One could say that information should start a flow of energy. SqEME® uses the terms *Chemistry*.

Building blocks and patterns for the structuring of processes

With the rise of rationalism, a traditional way of examining organizations has been to adopt the concept that in order to comprehend a complex system, one has to divide a problem into sub-problems, for as long as is necessary until there is just a single issue left that can be handled. There is not much to say against this method, other than that one loses sight of the interconnection of the parts, whilst their relation can actually be a part of the explanation as to why something either works or not. The traditional methods of research were particularly intended to reduce complexity. As our 'calculators' got more powerful, we could handle a greater complexity, but this did not lead to a larger insight in the coherence. Taylorism or Scientific Management

---

[26] Weick, K. E. (1996). Sensemaking in organizations. Newbury Park, CA: Sage
[27] Louis, Raymond (2006). Custom Kanban: Designing the System to Meet the Needs of Your Environment. University Park, IL: Productivity Press. ISBN 978-1-56327-345-2.

focused mainly upon splitting up, specializing and standardizing, whilst modern production control systems made this much less necessary, and required integration more than specialization. SqEME® Process Management focuses much less on detailing the descriptions of processes and pays more attention to the decision loops. The idea is that every process is unique and that it will never show itself in exactly the same form. Besides, any process has its own natural fluctuations. As anyone who learns to ride a bicycle has to discover, cycling requires a certain amount of balancing and leaning and, when one tries to correct it, this will result in a fall.

SqEME® regards descriptions mainly as tools that enable the recognition of a pattern; in combination with performance indicators this might possibly trigger an intervention, but if things are going well, then a signal will indicate 'all O.K.' so that the management should absolutely not intervene. In fact, workflow management is nothing more than recognition of patterns, and production control systems are based on earlier discovered patterns to ensure that processes take place in a certain way.

Certain certification models, such as ISO 9000, require that processes are described. The SqEME® method can be convenient for this, especially when the desire is to reduce the description of processes to the absolutely minimum necessary. Also with a holistic approach, or perhaps especially as a result of this, there is not only the need to recognize the different parts, but also the need to know what the performance indicators are (or should be) to get the whole to function properly. Armed with this knowledge, one can monitor whether the system functions properly, recognize possible hiccups or maybe discover opportunities for improvement. Measuring the heartbeat, blood pressure and the body temperature does not explain how our body operates, but it does indicate its condition. The condition of organizations will usually be measured by a series of performance indicators including financial levels, product quality, process time, use of material and consumption of energy, etc. Apart from this, users of the EFQM/INK management model are confronted with the question: 'Who is monitoring our processes apart from ourselves?', in other words: 'Who are our stakeholders?' and with the question: 'Which performance criteria do they use?' It might be wise to adopt the performance criteria they think are important in our own set of performance indicators and perhaps it could even be necessary to adjust our way of identifying business processes to reflect this. The concepts of performance indictors and process descriptions are gathered under the terms Correspondence.

The professionally mature employee as a starting point

For SqEME®, organizations are in the first place people. The quality of the organization is determined by the quality of the individual employee and the ability of the employee to cooperate with others to a large extent. For this, SqEME® uses the concept of professional maturity. Professional maturity is a key concept of the flexible organization. However, professional maturity is not a combination of words that one can find in a dictionary. It is a combination of the word professional and the word mature, that indicates skills, experience and competence of the employee, as well as a form of grown-up and committed with common values. A professionally mature employee is someone who is able to oversee the consequences of his own acts and who dares to deviate from rules when there are grounds for that. An important prerequisite is that the knowledge and skills necessary to execute the various tasks are present. SqEME® recognizes the principles of 'tacit knowledge' and 'explicit knowledge' (Polanyi), where tacit knowledge is the non-explicit (or almost non-explicit) knowledge and experience of someone, that is often regarded as a proof of craftsmanship, whilst explicit knowledge is the knowledge and experience that can be written down. Managers often strongly feel the need to register all knowledge and experience that is present, and deny that this is either impossible or requires an extreme effort. Apart from the fact that this urge ignores the fact that every human being is a unique personality, it can also be regarded threatening or offending. Writing down the operational procedures can suggest that there is a doubt about the presence of the knowledge needed for perform the work properly. It can be interpreted as an act of mistrust. It can also lead to thoughts that this knowledge is being deliberately held back by someone looking after their own interests. These are hardly the starting points that match the principles of inclusive thinking. When one assumes that every process takes place in a slightly different way each time, one has to ask oneself whether the efforts and the risks being run by the urge to document everything counterbalance the expected benefit[28].

SqEME® assumes that processes are performed by professionals or professionally mature employees, or that it pays to approach people in the organization as professionally mature employees. The selection on the basis of professional maturity or professionalism, or bringing employees to that level is, in this view, a crucial supportive process. As mentioned, the same professionally mature employees or professionals must have the necessary means and resources at their disposal. Knowing the structure of the organization and their place in it can be seen as a part of that; they must know who are their (internal) clients and suppliers and what their tasks and responsibilities are.

The latter should be undertaken in a manner that supports the focus of creating a process-driven organization so it will not 'slide off' to a classical hierarchical organization, in which knowing tasks and responsibilities is regarded as sufficient. Describing who the actors are and what means and facilities they have at their disposal belongs to the domain of Construction in the SqEME® approach.

2.3 SqEME® and EFQM

Although SqEME® was developed at an earlier date than European Business Excellence or the EFQM model it looks as if SqEME® is made for addressing the area of 'processes'. The EFQM model was first announced in 1992 as a reference model for selecting the winner of the European Quality Award. Almost immediately it became a popular framework for self assessment and benchmarking, not least because presenting a self assessment became a requisite for competing for the European Quality Award. For many organizations all over the world the EFQM model became the basis for their quality management, including those organizations who had not intention of competing for the award. Nowadays EFQM is one of the three important quality management approaches, if not the most important, alongside the American Malcolm Baldrige Quality Award criteria and the Japanese Deming Prize.

---

[28] This can be different for hazardous processes in which certain limits should absolutely not be exceeded. Think of nuclear fission processes in atomic power plants and of critical performance indicators as a part of diagnostic feedback systems that differ from persuasive systems coupled to values and interactive feedback systems under conditions of strategic uncertainties.

EFQM thinks from the (quality) management paradigm of *Continuous Improvement* in much the same way as SqEME®. They are non-prescriptive but describe the current situation in order to get an initial insight. This insight forms the basis for critical review and improvement: how is the work done (Do), what we learn from it (Check), what improvements can be made (Act), does the work function as (re)described (Plan) and so on. Because of the non-descriptiveness of both EFQM as SqEME®, they do not fit very well within the *Control* paradigm, although they are not useless. The criteria however are not supplied by the framework but are instead found in the description of the organization along the lines of the EFQM and/or SqEME® framework. For the paradigm *Breakthrough* other management models are more appropriate. For the paradigm *Reaching the Essence*, both EFQM and SqEME® are based on the same philosophy but are not exclusively searching for the fundamental concepts of the organization. With the help of the constitution window, SqEME® probably does this more effectively then the EFQM model.

Processes are at the heart of the EFQM model and this is not by accident. The basic idea of the developers of the model was that we need to look at organizations from another perspective. The ideas of Weick that one should not speak in terms of organizations but rather in terms of organizing, is embraced here. This concept of Weick can also be recognized within SqEME®. Instead of understanding organization in terms of tasks and responsibilities, you need to look at what is happening to the processes. The EFQM model is an input/output model, which is also the method used for working out the different windows of SqEME® as one can particularly see in the way that the Constitution and Correspondence windows are worked out. But it is not only the emphasis on process management makes the fit between SqEME® and the EFQM model. It is also the Rhineland value system that both share. It should be emphasised that the EFQM model was intended as an alternative for the Malcolm Quality Award, not for having something European, but for having an alternative to the Anglo-Saxon value system, focusing on stakeholder value instead of shareholder value, with increased emphasis on processes, weighted 20 % instead of 8.5 % as in the Malcolm Baldrige Award. It is interesting to note that the whole area of addressing 'key performance results' in the EFQM was the latest to be added, whilst the first was *process management* which was subsequently shortened to *processes* only.

In SqEME® result-oriented management is one of the basic principle, and results are equally important in the EFQM model. The EFQM model incorporates four areas on the right hand side of the model that are called the result areas, but in the way the model is drawn one can conclude that every area to be addressed is a 'result area' from the perspective of SqEME® . *People, policy & strategy* and *partnerships & resources* in the EFQM model are the inputs for the 'result area' *processes*, which in turn is a 'result area' that delivers input for people results, customer results and society results. Here, there is an important addition to the EFQM model. The model is based on the assumption that within each area to be addressed, each box is related to the other but it is unclear in what way. Because SqEME® explicitly investigates what is happening between the different 'result areas' with the help of the Chemistry window, where the focus is on messages ands message specification, it can be seen as a great addition to the EFQM model. The Chemistry window makes explicit all kinds of communication aspects, of which the EFQM model only addresses in general terms. One of the basic principles of SqEME® is the way in which information supply is viewed as an incentive for horizontal organizing.

EFQM, using a Rhineland management approach, focuses on the concept of stakeholder value instead of only on shareholder value. In the EFQM model, the stakeholders have an important but also somewhat ambiguous position. Firstly, *customer satisfaction, people satisfaction, impact on society* and *key performance results* together form the 'results' part of the model, whilst *leadership, people, policy & strategy, partnerships & resources* and *processes* are the 'enablers'. However, t they also form the input for 'innovation and learning'. So achieving results is not enough, they also have to be measured in such a way that they form the input for the enablers, in much the same way as the messages do in SqEME®.

Through using the results as input for different stakeholders, one is able to understand how the stakeholders experience these result. If you are able to appreciate the value that they get out of these results, you can then (re)design the processes of the organization in such a way that the desired results that have been formulated as part of the policy and strategy of the organization can be achieved. For that reason 'inclusive thinking' is an important principle, and it is in this area that SqEME® has made an important contribution to EFQM where this is currently included but is made nowhere near as explicit as is the case in SqEME®.

By describing an organization with the help of the EFQM model one more or less sees that it is made up of different building blocks. Using this description for self assessment and benchmarking as the EFQM organization advocates, follows the same principles of SqEME® where the identification and understanding of structured processes is one of their basic principles.

In the EFQM model particular importance is given to the workers in the organization. In the Anglo-Saxon philosophy the workers are the most important *resources* of the organization. For that reason human resource management is one of the most important criteria of the Malcolm Baldrige Quality Award. *Partnership & Resources* is an area that should be addressed in the EFQM model (with *information* as an important sub area to consider remembering that information supply as an incentive for horizontal organizing is one of the key principles of SqEME®), but humans are not in there. *People* is included in the EFQM model a separate area to address. The ideas behind this is that an organization is a conglomerate of people, and together they are the organization. In other words the people are the building blocks of an organization (well selected, trained, motivated, rewarded and, if necessary, removed) and therefore cannot own themselves as one can own a resource. One of the principles of SqEME® is the concept of the professional mature employee or the skilful worker as a starting point, and this fits in very well with the idea of having *People Management* as an area to address in the EFQM model.

In conclusion, for those organization who are applying the EFQM model, the SqEME® methodology it fits in very well as it also provide the organization with additional concepts that are either lacking or are only implicitly present in the EFQM model. SqEME® and EFQM share the paradigm of continuous improvement and both the embrace the Rhineland business philosophy. The basic principles of SqEME®: result-oriented management in the context of inclusive thinking and open system thinking, information supply as an incentive for horizontal organizing, building blocks and patterns for the structuring of processes, the professionally mature employee as a starting point, are all not only present in the EFQM model in some form, in some instances they also provide a valuable addition.

2.4   SqEME® for architecting the enterprise

The term architecture is overrunning the field of management. The fact that it appears as though architecting as phenomenon for managing an enterprise has blown over from the domain of Information Technology is the primary reason why there are some reservations about using the term for addressing process modelling and management activities. The reasons for being rather reticent about adapting the terminology are because architecture has a rather technological connotation. Architecting IT systems is about managing the complexity of designed, developed and implemented TECHNICAL systems. The behaviour of such systems is presumed to be predictable. However, SOCIAL systems, which are how SqEME views organizations, differ significantly from technical systems. Social systems have humans and their behaviour and, as a consequence, the phenomenon of unpredictability as a starting point! From that context, at first sight 'architecting an enterprise' looks like a self-contradiction.

Having stated this first reaction, it is obvious that, when accepting the phenomenon of unpredictability and human centeredness in the field of management, the use of (implicit) concepts of architecture can be extremely profitable. In fact it is the adoption of these architectural concepts that have made the use of the SqEME approach such a success. These concepts were already there, but were never described as being 'architectural'.

The IT field is familiar with the concept of 'chunkizing': dividing an object of interest into different chunks. In the IT field this is not done by defining closed boundaries around the chunks, but by defining the sockets and connectors in between the different chunks. This concept is the same as was mentioned earlier when describing the starting point of organizations as 'open and social systems'[29]: managing the boundary conditions!

TOGAF™[30] as an open standard Architecture Framework emphasizes the use of the concept of an Enterprise Continuum to reflect different levels of abstraction in an architecture development process. This same continuum is also addressed in section 3.1 where we mention the various levels of abstraction for managing processes.
Another very interesting concept within TOGAF™ and other Architecture Frameworks is that of 'reusability'. Through the use of the four windows, in particular the windows focusing upon the Constitution and the Construction of the enterprise, the use of the SqEME approach leads to the description of reusable building blocks as more generally recognizable Key Result Areas, as well as specific resources for executing the detailed activities required to comply with the agreements.

For all of these reasons, the SqEME approach could be described as an Architecture Framework. Nevertheless, it is worth noting that, for example, the Architecture Development Method (ADM) within TOGAF™ , as with other Architecture Frameworks, evidently has its roots in a technical system perspective. This method doesn't pay much attention to the fact that discussing, describing and learning about the working of the organization as a social system can, as a result of the growing consciousness of the participants, directly lead to changed working methods, without the need to plan and implemen the ' migration'.

---

[29] Emery, F. & Trist, E. (1965). The causal texture of organizational environments
[30] The Open group Architecture Framework TOGAF™

Maybe in further editions, when the thinking about organizations as social systems becomes more widely accepted, the SqEME approach will be publicly described as an architectural approach by changing its identity to something along the lines of, for example: The SqEME Architecture Framework for Process Oriented Organizations.

3 Process Management and the SqEME® Approach

3.1 Process Management, Working ON the Organization

In this book, we join the tradition of Quality Management, of which Juran – amongst others - is the founder. In the SqEME® approach, process management stands for making the organization fit for use. In other words, process management is about the design and continuous improvement of the organization. Process management has to enable people to 'take a step back' from the daily hectic state and to understand what is really happening. They then need to share the big picture and come to agreements about cooperation. It is always remarkable to see how often there is no time for things that are considered really important. Every company will, at a certain stage, be confronted with the need to work on quality. Too often this is related to overdue maintenance and emergency measures (i.e. a reorganization). SqEME® Process management emphasizes the fact that working on the quality of the organization, through sharing views and coming to agreements, has to be a structural activity.

Processes in the organization have always been given an important role by the quality tradition. Organizations working with the EFQM Excellence Model will endorse that process management represents the heart of this model: no result without a process. Process management forms a bridge between the so-called enablers and the results. Reciprocally, the results give cause for reconsidering aspects of the organization. In this way, the model works as a 'Plan Do Check Adapt cycle'. People in the organization are stimulated to continuously work on the improvement of the organization. The application of the EFQM Excellence Model within an enterprise contributes significant to the understanding of process management. Many companies have described their processes. The managers in those companies have become aware that processes often go beyond and above departments and have for that reason assigned process owners. Apart from describing their processes, they also started improving them.

Apart from the models mentioned, a number of standards are of great value to quality management. ISO 9000 for quality, ISO 14000 for environment, safety and health legislation for the employees and sector-standards like HKZ for healthcare. These standards also have the Plan Do Check Adapt cycle as their basis, which makes process management an important provision. Companies working towards certification on the basis of these standards have often taken processes as a starting point and incorporated them in their operational management. Many companies have described and implemented their quality, environmental or safety management systems (either separately or combined) through processes.

A characteristic of quality thinking is the level of abstraction at which process management is approached. In the European study of quality management 'The European Way to Excellence' three levels of abstraction have been described in order to understand the working of the organization[31]. These levels of abstraction have been called 'framing', 'alignment' and 'deployment'. The level of abstraction in the quality tradition is the 'alignment' of the organization. This is the level at which mission, vision and strategy are translated into the way in which the organization has been designed, i.e. the level of abstraction at which one determines how the operation should take place. This level of abstraction is also called working ON the organization. Complementary to this, we find the operational level, the workers in their hectic daily activities. On this level of deployment one works WITH the organization[32].

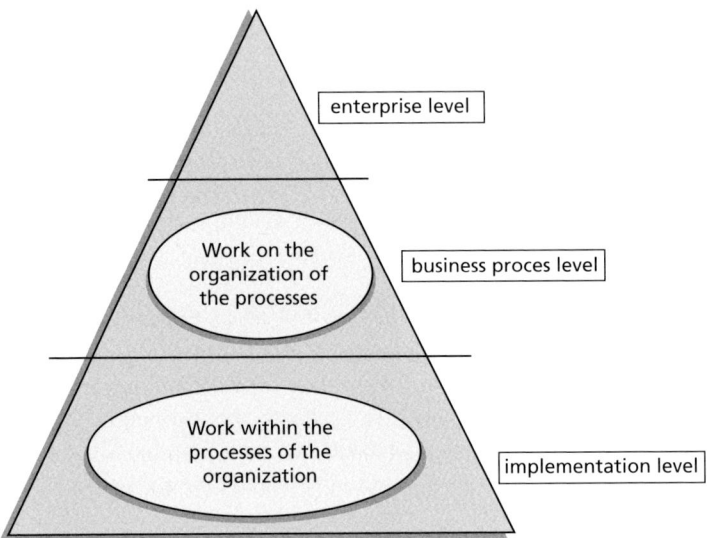

Figure 3.1   The various levels of abstraction for managing processes

In this vision, process management is about working on the quality of the processes of the enterprise. Alongside the perspective of assurance, it includes the perspective of continuous improvement. By placing the alignment of the organization in the light of continuous improvement, this level can also be addressed as 'maintaining' the organization.

3.2   Processes, the Verbs of the Organization

When talking to people about their work, it is interesting to observe the words they use. Often, one is inclined to talk about positions or departments. It is better to focus their verbs. 'we conquer crime', 'we produce semi-manufactured articles', 'we organize day-trips', 'we repair cars'. In an abstract form, processes can be regarded as the verbs of the organization. In the example

---

[31] Hardjono, Ten Have and Ten Have (1996), The European Way to Excellence
[32] With thanks to former *INK*-chairman Prof. Drs. Frans Stevens

used in this book of the car company, the processes, for example, are 'purchasing', 'preparing' and 'selling'. In order to address this properly, one needs nouns like 'purchase contracts', 'sales contracts', 'maintenance reports', completed where necessary with 'suppliers lists' and 'market information'. Commonly used verbs, combined with the common nouns, yield a 'pattern' of working. This pattern is the object of interest in redesigning the organization. The pattern of working provides a view of the essence of the organization. Trading cars on basis of a specific client's request will be organized differently to bulk trade. In patterns like this, the nouns are of great significance. Nouns represent the results in the organization and, as a consequence, they form the basis of the messaging, the chemistry of the enterprise. In other words, at this level of abstraction, information is seen as a representation of the result achieved. Messages are about a concept an 'event' or a new situation.

The 'work order' in the car company [garage, motor shop] represents the result of the agreement with the client and the 'repair report' relates to the repaired car.

To view processes at this level of abstraction has the great advantage that they can be discussed as if they form the building blocks of the enterprise. Clusters of verbs and nouns are the essentials to express the way in which professionals provide results on the basis of their craftsmanship, good communication and useful resources. Because the building blocks do not describe any aspects of implementation, they should be recognizable for people from different organizations.

The understanding of processes from this level of abstraction becomes exchangeable, so other departments or related organizations can learn from each other's way of working, or they can be connected to improve their mutual cooperation or the wider supply chain cooperation. If processes are viewed as the building blocks that provide results in response to specific client needs, then the level of abstraction can provide the capability to see the enterprise in its entirety and provide the opportunity to identify improvements where the quality of the operation can really be influenced.

3.3 Describing Processes

As soon as the processes in organizations are discussed, a question frequently (if not always) asked is: 'up to which level of detail do you work out processes and do you also need to work out all exceptions?'. The SqEME® method has a clear rule for working out this process architecture. SqEME® Process Management states that this question should be lifted up to the level of abstraction where it belongs: that is designing, engineering and maintaining the organization. Process architecture is all about working on processes, in which the processes are regarded as the building blocks of the enterprise. Process management is the 'art of abstracting'. The initial condition for process management is that everyone in the organization is able to think in terms of processes. An organization that wants to control their operational management (their processes) and wants to improve them continuously, will first have to know what the processes are, how they work together and how they influence each other. We call this the process architecture. Whatever the reason for working on the quality of the organization might be (as described above), the starting point will always be the description of this process architecture.

Key to describing processes is understanding the desirable operating procedure. Often one looks deeper and writes down someone's skills. We call this the 'white box' approach. Looking through the Correspondence window, one focuses on the performance. The building block is 'forced open' and made transferable. Often this happens by means of process descriptions.

A service organization had a problem concerning the quality of the work performed. As a solution they sent all twelve engineers 'to the moors' (Dutch expression for outdoor teambuilding) to once and for all agree the standard operating procedures. The engineers came back to work enthusiastic, carrying a pile of paper. All procedures were worked out, duplicated, plasticized and added to the gear in their service vehicles. What became apparent after a while? The quality of work had improved significantly, but a glance at the interior of the vans proved that the documents had either been lost already, or they were retrieved from some corner in their original state. After an evaluation, the company concluded that the value of the session at the moors was mainly to be found in the exchange of knowledge between the engineers and not in the paperwork. Now, they annually organize a similar session, and they no longer use the term 'standard operating procedures', but instead use 'good practice'.

Process management according to the 'white box' approach is about knowing the activities and the risks in detail and, after that, providing the necessary means to support the professional executing the work. The 'white box' approach assumes processes are predictable (or that they are only slightly uncertain) so it becomes possible to map the progress of the processes. The illustration above shows that everyone working on process descriptions in principle learns from doing this. This also implies that organizations that delegate the writing down of processes to their quality department, or outsource them, do not profit from the learning experience. The 'appearances' of the 'white box' approach are tuned to practice on the work floor; job descriptions, posters, stickers, screens, plasticized cards, etc. Process descriptions are, so to speak, in the example of the car company, what the mechanic takes with him under the car to assist him in doing his job. SqEME® Process Management states that the 'white box' approach has a maximum added value if the operations are critical. E.g. when legislation sets preconditions for the type of work, or when it concerns high-risk activities or work related to specific incidents. With the exception of these jobs, processes do not have to be written down into detail. The correct execution of the job does not occur spontaneously but requires a lot of experience, background knowledge and it asks for the mutual transfer of knowledge between employees. Apart from resources, training and education are essential aids.

Another perspective on the describing of processes is the so-called 'black box' approach. The following quote by De Bono about the potato peeling machine is helpful in illustrating the perception of a process as a black box of the organization:
'When young children are being asked to invent a potato peeling machine, they draw a long tube through which the potatoes fall into a box, with the simple note: 'In here the potatoes get peeled'.
Another tube releases the peeled potatoes. There is nothing mysterious about this box, as De Bono says: 'It just performs the potato peeling function'[34]. Describing processes from this perspective is about 'designing' operational process in response to the required cooperation. The description signifies that there is a long way to go in terms of specifying the content of the work,

---

[34] De Bono (1969), The Mechanism of Mind, p.17.

and that the focus is more on the interconnection of the processes and at the way professionals cooperate. Process descriptions coming from a 'black box' approach should be seen as a means to record the agreements about this cooperation. In the example of De Bono, the agreements were about the tubes instead of agreements about the content of the box. The power of process descriptions for the design and development of processes following the 'black box' approach is in an unambiguous framework of terms, the language for the description of the management model in recognizable verbs and nouns. In order to arrive at agreements about cooperation it is necessary for these professionals to really share the same descriptions when it concerns working on the quality of the organization. The 'black box' approach gives elbow room for 'creativity' and 'flexibility', but also the responsibility to provide the right amount of space to these professionals. This means that the professional should be given the right authority to do his job and be supplied with the appropriate means to do so.

In daily practice, these 'white box' and 'black box' approaches cannot work without each other. For any organization that wants to invest in their processes, the application of both approaches has to be balanced for each building block, rather than choosing one instead of the other. The key is to balance their respective use, rather than a choice of one against the other. Does one want to have emphasis on the content of the work, the craftsmanship, or merely on the interconnection of the professionals, on improving the level of cooperation?. The latter is also referred to as the horizontal organization. Above all it is true that the organization is a collection of cooperating professionals. These professionals provide results via a shared ambition, on the basis of their craftsmanship, good communication and practical means. Applying both approaches simultaneously is the natural tension one has to deal with. Managing processes conceals the challenge of finding the right balance between 'ordering' professionals and workers self-control[35].

3.4 Working on the Development of the Organization

When working on the quality of processes, the starting point is the organization as a 'social system'. The operation either stands or falls with the correct approach to the interplay of the -professionally mature- employees. It requires the right balance between structure, corporate culture and management style.

Developing the organization requires investment in these three pillars. The structure – the formal agreements that are the basis for cooperation, the corporate culture – the unwritten rules of the game as they have grown or 'bedded in' over time, and the management style - the manner in which the enterprise is governed and the behaviour of its leaders; these three are the points of attention when improving the organization as a whole[36].

In the first place, the SqEME® method for designing the management model requires attention for the (horizontal) structure of the organization. This means actively walking along the four windows that are covered in the following chapters. In essence, this is an activity of 'ordering'. The

---

[35] Juran (1951), Juran's Quality Control Handbook
[36] Peter Scott-Morgan (1994), The Unwritten Rules of the Game

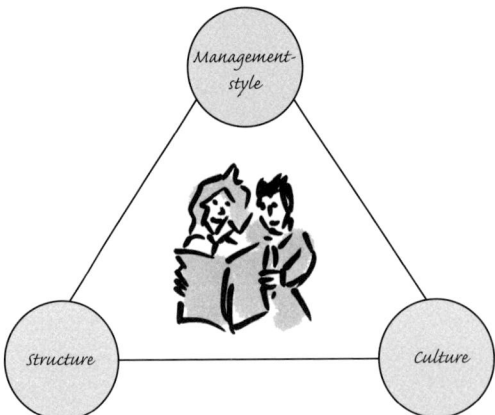

Figure 3.2   The organization as a social system and the three pillars for organizational development

paradigm in this is that working on the structure of the processes, from a social system perspective, ultimately influences the management style and the corporate culture of the organization. This requires a thorough investigation and coaching when looking through the four windows. Why do we see what we see, what are the underlying beliefs, how do we associate with each other on these matters? We have to keep an eye on the balance between the three pillars.

3.5   Architectural Approach: Language and Signs

Applying the SqEME® method makes it easier to communicate the design of the organization. On the basis of strict conventions the essence of the social system is structured. In a technical sense, the SqEME® method can be compared to the method used by an architect who is preparing a design for the radical rebuilding of a house. He draws rooms and floors, sketches the paths between them, indicates building materials, incorporates facilities like electricity and piping for water, etc. With a limited number of symbols and models he can unambiguously lay down the design. Technically, the SqEME® method is just a set of symbols with which to model the business architecture. But beware: adopting this view means that process management can easily be seen as a technical exercise, in which the processes are just written down and then dictated.

Process management using the SqEME® method is something that concerns all people in the organization. The SqEME® method assumes that working on the quality of the organization in principle is a task of every employee. Everyone is, as it were, the architect of the organization, or can be so. So the techniques of describing will not just be used by one architect, but they are a means to work together on the processes of the organization. In this chapter, we have already become acquainted with the level of abstraction of working on the organization. Who the workers on the organization are completely depends on the way the organization has been designed and the perspective one has of organizing. The old perspective is that working on the organization is a task laid down with management. Managers are the people who have the view over the organization as a whole, so they can control the functioning of the organization. Many organizations are still governed in this way. A number of specific tasks are allocated to staff like the quality manager, the controller, or in some organizations with the ICT department.

However, the SqEME® approach starts from the principle that, just like in leadership, these tasks can be claimed by anyone in the organization. Process management is not necessarily linked to the vertical hierarchical structure of the organization. It is primarily to be found in the value system and the passion of the people.

Implicitly, these 'process roles' are always present in organizations. They appear either formally or informally. The role can be picked up by process owners or by structures of consultation. Even a 'role' like quality manager can, in some cases, be justified. In this case, line management delegates the authority to others in the organization when it is concerned with the working on the organization.

In order to do this properly, one needs a common 'language'. In its methodology, SqEME® Process Management provides the organization with such a language and a set of signs (conventions) with which to define the descriptions and the agreements. In this way, process management becomes a tool for everyone in the organization, facilitating cooperation in order to realize continuous improvement. The organization puts the professional at the centre.

3.6   Conventions for Language and Signs

When applied to process management, the SqEME® method offers four windows in which models can be distinguished for describing the processes. With these descriptions (images of the complex reality), one wants to answer a set of questions, defined beforehand, in an unambiguous way to the user. A model is a complete, concise and consistent description of an object of interest which is designed for a particular reason. That reason, called the 'purpose' of the model, by definition answers a set of questions. In this way, the holistic model presents the opportunity to various target groups in the organizations. Such groups are offered the opportunity to approach the organization from different levels of abstraction by means of the holistic model. The SqEME® method distinguishes eight models for the design and maintenance of the process architecture of an organization. It is important that these models are consistent with each other. In addition to the SqEME® models, other models can also be used, or variations can be made to the SqEME® models, as long as the paradigm of consistency is not violated and the correct target group identify themselves with the models.

Process management according to the Constitution window stands for the overview. It is about sharing views between people in the enterprise on what the enterprise stands for and how it is built up. Acquiring a common understanding of the 'big picture'. How are mission and vision translated in the Key Result Areas of the enterprise? How are these building blocks interconnected? What outcomes do these building blocks have, represented through the information supply between professionals? These essential structures cross right through the well known organizational structure, the departments detailed in the organization scheme.
The schema's that are used for showing the views through the Constitution window are:
• *The Enterprise Architecture*: a suprastructure of the organization, answering the questions relating to what the main Key Result Areas of the organization are. Do these building blocks, which are the essential verbs of the enterprise, match the mission, vision and strategy of the enterprise?

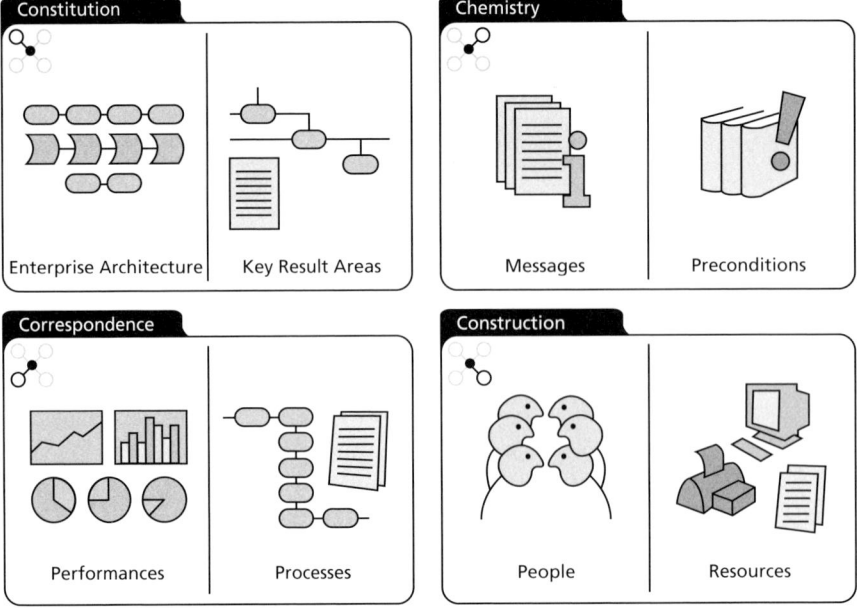

Figure 3.3   The set of symbols of the SqEME® method

- *The Key Result Areas*: Activity (Interaction) Diagrams that answer the questions on what the relationships are between the different Key Result Areas, together with the constituent activities and messages of the enterprise.

Process management looking through the Chemistry window is about the collaboration of people and their commitments, and about connecting their actions. It is about the company as a community of professionals. It can be summarised as *coherence* and *interplay*. In this model, the starting point is the messaging within the organization. The agreements about the quality of the messages can be characterized as the minimal 'briefings' that professionals in the organization require in order to fulfil their tasks. What information do I need in order to do my work properly? It is about the interaction between workers, their 'speech acts'[37]. What information that others are dependent upon, within or outside the organization, do I need to communicate?

A message is seen as the representation of a certain (intermediate) result. By laying down agreements about these messages, the collaboration can be designed. In this, information is specifically a social 'thing'. People in the company have to be willing to share data. And, last but not least, attention should be paid to the meaning of this data; the semantic interoperability, the quality of the communication between the transmitter and the receiver. It would be easier if an enterprise was like 'one semantic community', but in practice that's never the case. Much effort is needed to frame a universal and unambiguous meaning of data. This is needed to improve the collaboration between professionals who may have very different backgrounds, for example because of different levels of education.

---

[37]   John Langshaw Austin: How to Do Things With Words. Cambridge (Mass.) 1962 - Paperback: Harvard University Press, 2nd edition, 2005, ISBN 0-674-41152-8.

What data do I need to distribute to other people in or outside the enterprise that they are dependent upon? Do they extract the right meaning from that data? The quality of the enterprise depends on the quality of the communication between the professionals. Investing in this aspect of the enterprise is, in open system terms, called 'Managing the boundary conditions'.

The models to show the chemistry between processes are:
- *The message specifications:* mini-contracts between professionals about the sharing of information, answering the question of how collaboration can be made verifiable.
- *Preconditions:* an analysis matrix answering the question of whether the organization is 'compliant', offering a grasp of the issue that relates to acquiring a 'license to operate'.

Process management according to the Construction window is about deployment. Process management covers the implementation of processes via the assignment of tasks, distribution of responsibilities and authority, and definition, development and implementation of the resources (templates, ICT, work orders, training) that are deemed necessary for professionals to be able to perform their tasks properly. The models used for Construction are:
- *People:* matrices specifying the complete range of tasks, responsibilities and authorities in the organization answering the question of who does what.
- *Resources:* matrices that give an insight into the availability of resources that are provided to employees in order to assist them in performing their tasks.

Process management according to Correspondence stands for monitoring the process: be it the desktop of the professional or the dashboard of the business manager. This viewing angle provides the detailed understanding of the business. This can be done in the form of short process charts in which the activities with their input and output are put in successive order. The goal of this is to control and to assure operational management. The models used for Correspondence are:
- *Process flowcharts:* flow charts for employees and process owners, answering the questions about which successive activities should be performed at which moment.
- *Scorecards:* the instruments that answer the questions about how the desired situation corresponds with reality and if objectives are met by performance indicators.

4 Constitution

The Constitution window focuses upon the basic principles and essence of the enterprise. When using the SqEME® method, this constitution is primarily based on the concept of the organization as a social system. The enterprise will be viewed as a collection of cooperating professionals. Through the use of the Constitution window, this social system is investigated in more detail. The window's most characteristic benefit is the way in which it reveals building blocks and working patterns. It provides a deeper level of significance. When the architecture of the enterprise changes, the basic essentials upon which the organization is based also change. This is why the Constitution window is intended to address the exchange and recording of the contemplative descriptions, in order to gain an insight into the essence of the changes and to think about the need, the use and the consequences of these changes. The activity of creating and discussing the descriptions is as important, or maybe even more important then the descriptions self. This has to do with the starting point of the inter-subjective truth and the earlier statements in this book that an organization isn't something tacit you can hold in your hand[38]. Whether the window is used in this way depends strongly on the maturity of the management, the management style adopted and the corporate culture.

The Constitution window investigates the essential characteristics of the enterprise. It answers the question of which is the most appropriate mission for the organization. A clear understanding of the constitution of the enterprise is needed for the professionals. This understanding will contribute to the alignment of their individual and common ambitions.

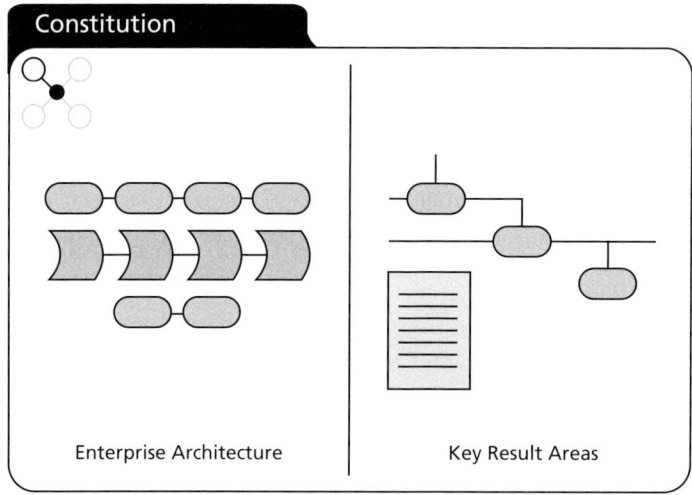

Figure 4.1   The Constitution window

---

[38] Weick, K. E. (1996). Sensemaking in organizations. Newbury Park, CA: Sage

In this, the architecture of the enterprise is an abstract model. It does not reveal how a company executes is processes. It deals with the aspect of 'what Result Areas are of major importance to the enterprise and with what activities the enterprise achieves these results'. Naming functions as Key Result Areas means identifying those building blocks of the enterprise that make an essential contribution to its business and should therefore be organized appropriately.

With the help of the Constitution window, the essentials of the enterprise are visualized. In this way the accent is on indicating the important business functions by describing the Key Result Areas and their (inter)relationships. The model of the constitution is built up from one central diagram of the Enterprise Architecture and the constituent diagrams of the Key Result Areas that focus on a description of the interconnected activities. The Constitution window provides a coherent view of all of the interrelated Result Areas and activities. In this manner, the model indicates the building blocks that the enterprise recognizes as being fundamental to realizing their mission, their vision and their strategy. The Constitution window displays the conceptualisation of the organization.

The Enterprise Architecture and the constituent activity diagrams neglect aspects of construction, deployment and implementation. Looking through this window, one does not bother about what the organization looks like in its daily operation. Things such as who does the work, with what information, or according to what guidelines, etc, have no effect on the view through the Constitution window. These are just extended diagrams and specifications that come into view through the other windows of the SqEME® approach.

In the Constitution window, processes are seen as if they were the recognizable verbs (the Lego-blocks) of the organization. The manufacturing of a product, the preparations for a surgical operation in a hospital, or the ordering and delivery of a pizza are, in a sense, all examples of a chain of operationally interconnected building blocks.

A chain of building blocks can be compared to a train that is composed of separate wagons. Of course, for every wagon there are certain technical demands in its design, and boundary conditions that are adjusted to their meaning and actual use. The couplings have to take into account the possibility of 'hooking up' other wagons. A reliable coupling (or in other words good communication) between the coherent processes is a condition for an efficient use!

The Language and Signs of this window

The Constitution window uses a free format description of 'Enterprise Architecture' and then again strictly defined 'activity diagrams'. To enable a more detailed description of the drawing conventions and for examples, refer to section 4.6 (Tips & Tricks) and Appendix II. There is also a handy pocket guide, called 'Language and Signs'[39], issued by the SqEME® Foundation, that describes all the drawing conventions and supplies tips and examples. Parts of this pocket guide are integrated in this chapter.

---

[39] Van Velzen, Van Oosten, Snijders and Hardjono (2007), SqEME® Process Management – Language and Signs.

4.1   Developing a description of the Enterprise Architecture

An Enterprise Architecture is a picture that displays the essential building blocks of the enterprise, the important functions, or better - the Key Result Areas. Through this model an enterprise indicates which aspects are seen to be crucial for the achievement of their objectives. The power of the Enterprise Architecture lies in its ability to represent the essentials into a single 'big picture', which can then be used as the basis upon which the company can define and communicate their core activities. It is of great importance that this view is drawn up in cooperation with the employees of the company, in order to come to a shared view, a generally accepted ' big picture' in which the organization recognizes itself. The development of the Enterprise Architecture can be done in any arbitrarily selected form, as long as the Key Result Areas are recognizable. Later in the chapter, a car company, affiliated to a dealer organization is used as an example. The key activities of this company are the sale and maintenance of cars. At the same time as selling cars, used cars are also purchased. The core functions of this enterprise should be captured in the Enterprise Architecture. The diagram will often also show the functions relating to the governance, planning and improvement activities.

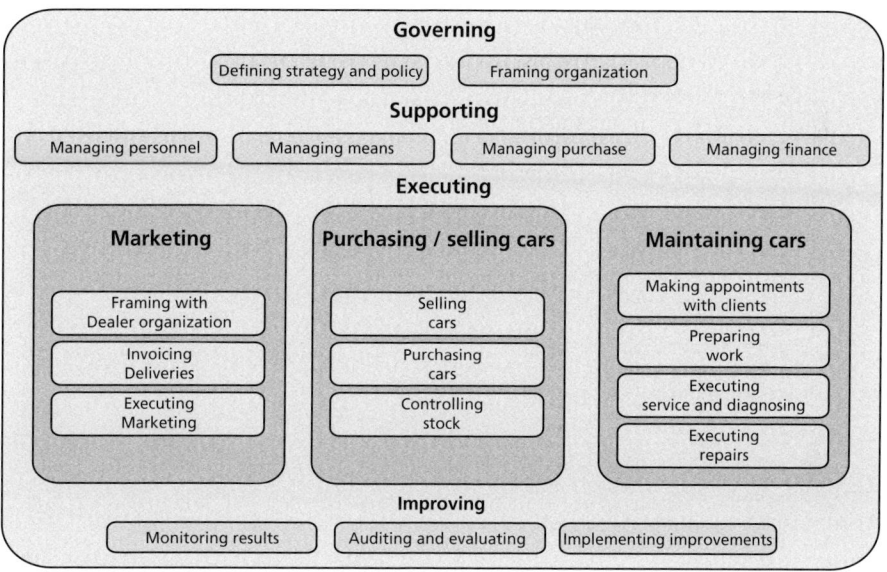

Example 1.   The Enterprise Architecture 'Car Company'.

4.2   Describing Key Result Areas

The Key Result Area description provides an insight into a distinctive part of the Enterprise Architecture, showing the constituent activities and the interactions between them. The conventions for describing Key Result Areas have been derived from Structured Analysis and Design Technique (SADT), also called IDEF0 (Integration Definition for Function Modelling). This technique was developed in the early seventies to help in the modelling of systems. Because of its layered and modular construction, one can coherently map and study the building blocks of the enterprise in a step-by-step approach. Starting from the investigation of the real operational processes and the communication between the people executing those processes, a coherent and abstract description can be formed of what these professionals are doing, and in what context. This is why verbs are used to indicate activities and nouns are used to define the interconnections, the context of those activities.

In a Key Result Area we draw the processes in the form of a box. Every box is identified with a verb. Arrows link the boxes together and represent the relationships between the activities in the sense of cross functional information, the briefings that the professionals responsible for undertaking the activities require. This means that the arrows represent the messaging within the organization, the interaction between the activities. In terms of the organization as a social system, the arrows represent the essential communication between the professionals in the organization.

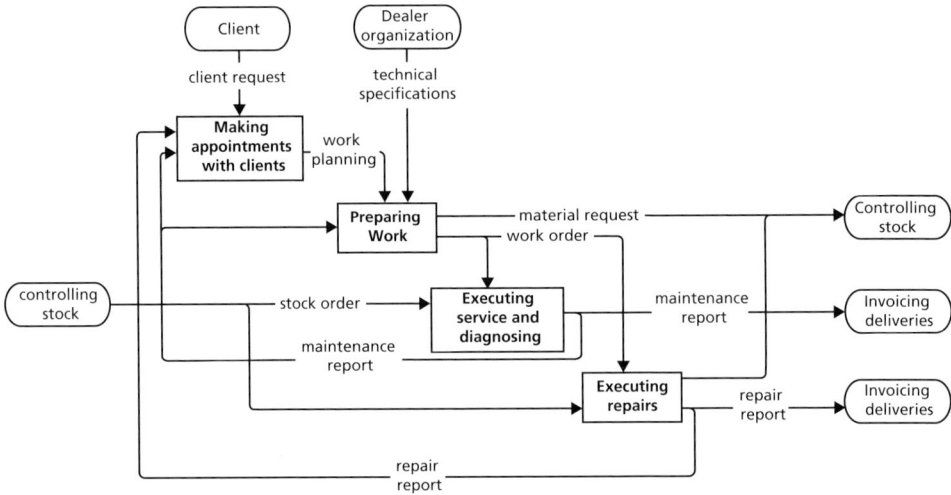

Example 2.   Key Result Area description 'Maintaning cars'.

Which people actually execute the activities within a process is a question that will not be answered by looking through the Constitution window. This will be examined through the Construction window.

The arrows in the diagrams represent the interaction between the activities. We call this messaging because an arrow stands for information-flow in any imaginable form. Think, for instance, of a form, a plan or computer data. There are three possible relationships that messages can have with boxes: an incoming message (input), a controlling message (control) and an outgoing message (output). Each of these relationships is represented by an arrow that is connected to one of the sides of a box.

According to the agreement, the left side of a box is meant for input arrows, the upper side is for control arrows and the right side is for output arrows.

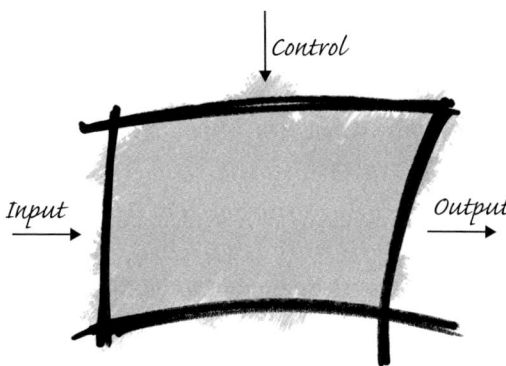

Figure 4.2   Framing activities

Output arrows are the messages that transfer information about the results and the decisions of the activity concerned. An outgoing message is a representation of the achieved result. In the activity diagrams that describe the Key Result areas of the car company, the car itself is never expressed by a symbol. The car can be recognized in specific messages concerning the state of the car. The repair report is a representation of the fact that the state of the car has changed, i.e. it has been repaired. The repair report in a car company serves both external parties and the internal processes like invoicing and the transfer of the car to the client.

Control arrows represent the messages that control and sometimes also trigger the process (triggering). On the basis of the content of a message like this, the output of the delivering process can be judged. Control areas set the boundaries of the activities. In this way, the work order in the car company will contain the description of the work to be done (with the agreement of the client) and any other preparatory activities in the process that might be necessary.

Input arrows represent the information to be accessed during the execution of the activity. In the case of the car company, one can imagine that the service history is consulted (input arrow) when making an appointment with a client.

Figure 4.3 shows the essential relationships between boxes and arrows, with a brief description of their meaning.

Consistency of the Architecture

When we describe different Key Result Areas, we must make sure that all diagrams and the activities they show are connected correctly, in order to obtain a consistent architecture. A description of a Key Result Area has external arrows, i.e. arrows that arrive at or come from the edges of the diagram. These arrows are the links between the Key Result Area concerned and the 'outside world'. To maintain the order and the coherence in the Enterprise Architecture as a whole, the relationships between the separately described Key Result Areas have to be mapped. At a higher level we can describe the interrelated Key Result Areas in a new diagram. As is obvious, diagrams of Key Result Areas can be 'nested'.

The subdividing of a Key Result Area is called decompositioning. The underlying diagram is called the child-diagram. This diagram describes the complete content of the box on top of it and the allied communication. It does not describe anything outside the boundaries of the box. The box that is being analysed is called the parent box, so the diagram in which this box is present is called the parent diagram. All external arrows of a child diagram have to be consistent with the displayed messages in the parent diagram.

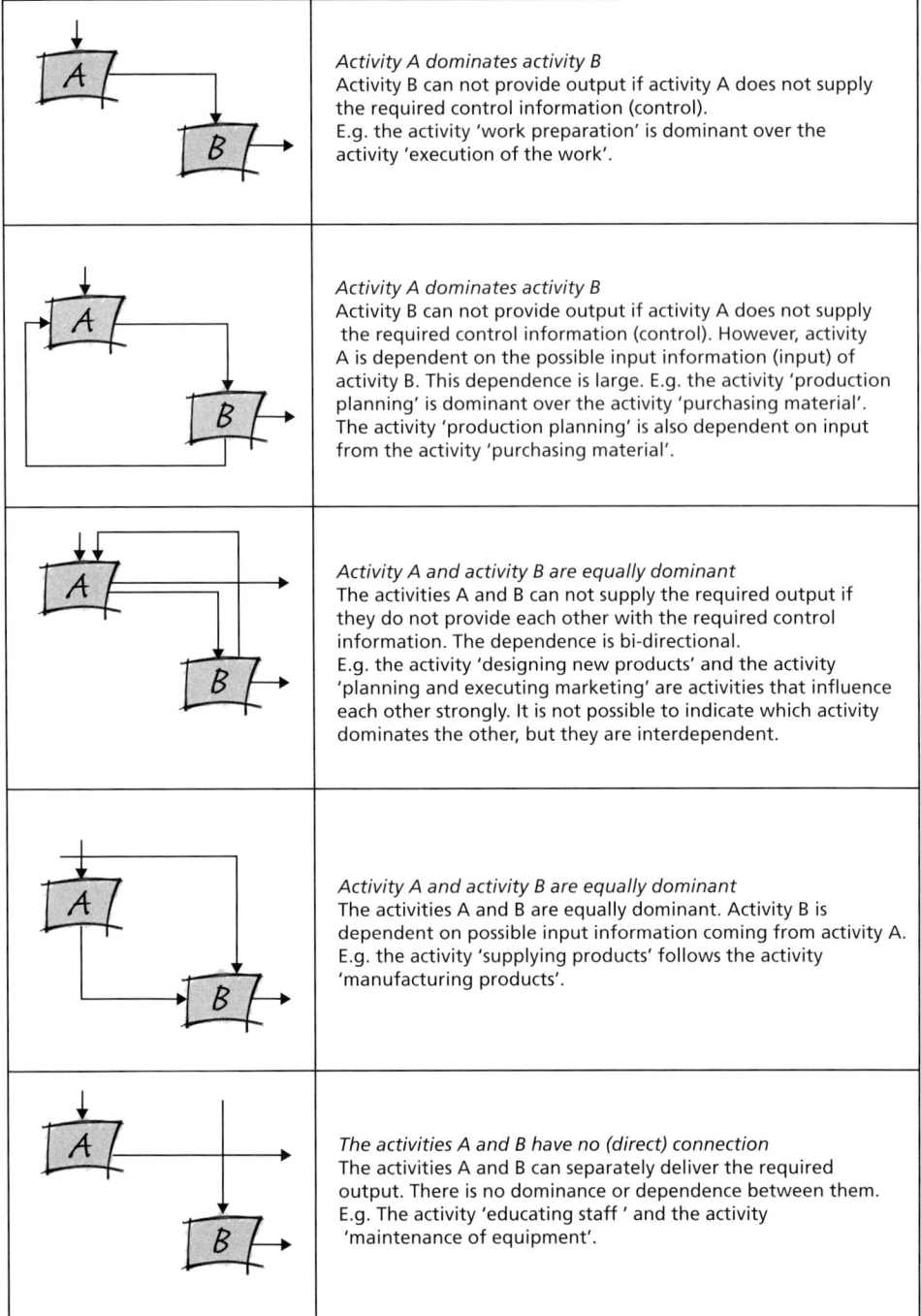

The table in the figure contains the following entries:

Diagram	Description
A → B	**Activity A dominates activity B** Activity B can not provide output if activity A does not supply the required control information (control). E.g. the activity 'work preparation' is dominant over the activity 'execution of the work'.
A ↔ B	**Activity A dominates activity B** Activity B can not provide output if activity A does not supply the required control information (control). However, activity A is dependent on the possible input information (input) of activity B. This dependence is large. E.g. the activity 'production planning' is dominant over the activity 'purchasing material'. The activity 'production planning' is also dependent on input from the activity 'purchasing material'.
A ⇄ B	**Activity A and activity B are equally dominant** The activities A and B can not supply the required output if they do not provide each other with the required control information. The dependence is bi-directional. E.g. the activity 'designing new products' and the activity 'planning and executing marketing' are activities that influence each other strongly. It is not possible to indicate which activity dominates the other, but they are interdependent.
A → B	**Activity A and activity B are equally dominant** The activities A and B are equally dominant. Activity B is dependent on possible input information coming from activity A. E.g. the activity 'supplying products' follows the activity 'manufacturing products'.
A B	**The activities A and B have no (direct) connection** The activities A and B can separately deliver the required output. There is no dominance or dependence between them. E.g. The activity 'educating staff' and the activity 'maintenance of equipment'.

Figure 4.3   Different interaction patterns between activities

The principle of bounding a box happens at all levels of the model. In this way a 'tree structure' is created, the 'hierarchical decomposition' with which we can manage the coherence and consistence of the Key Result Areas of the enterprise.

At the highest level, one box and several arrows are used to indicate the boundaries of the whole Enterprise Architecture. After all, as with any enterprise, their architecture, never exists in isolation. They always interact with their environment as an open system.

Whilst on this point, it is important to indicate where the enterprise ends and where the surroundings begin. An Enterprise Architecture, and also the description of a specific Key Result Area within it, limits its subject. The Constitution window maps the interconnected activities of the whole enterprise.

The arrows that are connected with the 'top level diagram' indicate the most important controls, inputs and outputs that form the formal interfaces of the enterprise with its environment.

At the bottom level, there is obviously no need for more detailed activity diagrams. Those activities are often modelled for a more detailed understanding, but then using the correspondence window, approaching those ' verbs' as processes, gives an insight into the constituent successive activities. For a better understanding of chains of activities like this and descriptions of them, see chapter 7.

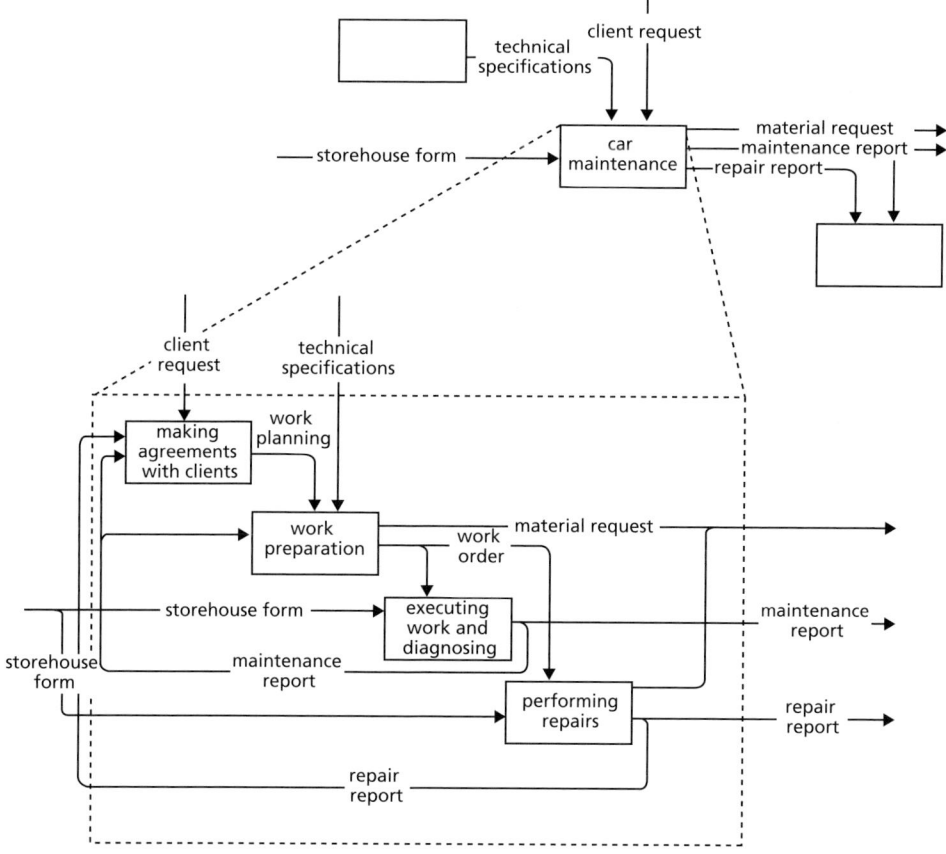

Figure 4.4   Mother-child relationship between Key Result Areas

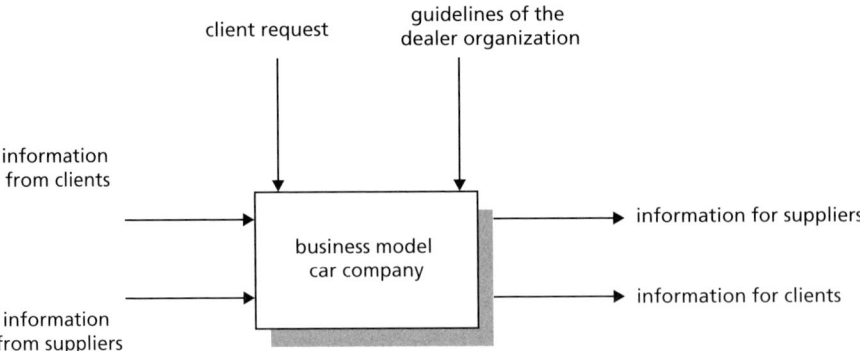

Example 3.   The top level for capturing the essence of the car company.

When creating and updating diagrams by hand, it is quite a task to keep the collection diagrams consistent with each other by means of numbering the information channels.

Fortunately, there are several computer applications that can perform the consistency checks of the models with little effort and completely free of errors.

4.3   The concept of Key Result Area, Activity and Process

Looking through the Constitution window we see the building blocks of the enterprise which we call Key Result Areas and the constituent activities. Where appropriate, an activity within a Key Result Area can also be addressed as a (Key) Result Area and made explicit with its own activity diagram.

The concept of a process in this book is, for consistency reasons, explicitly coupled to the Correspondence window. From that viewpoint we are interested to understand the behaviour of a process, defined as a chain of successive activities.

To be perfectly clear, when we are looking through the Constitution window, we will consequently use the word 'activity' and not 'process' for addressing the building blocks identified by a verb.

Both a Key Result Area and a process are composed of activities. The first addresses the interaction between activities, the messaging and information supply. The second focuses on the successive order, the time-based flow of activities. So be aware of the different meaning of the order setting of the building blocks and the connecting arrows in these two modelling techniques.

Here's an indication of the complexity we have to deal with: an activity defined in a Key Result Area description can be worked out as a process, breaking that activity up again into 'smaller' verbs, the successive activities of that process. But a process-flow diagram can also be used as a model to show the time-based order of activities, of which the interaction pattern is also modelled by means of a Key Result Area description.

In practice the use of the words 'activity' and ' process' will be mixed up. After all, an activity or even a Key Result Area can, at any time, be studied and defined as a process.

4.4 Developing the Understanding of the Constitution of the Enterprise

Added value of the constitution

Modelling the Enterprise Architecture and the constituent Key Result Areas is an intellectual exercise of which anyone might ask themself questions in terms of what's the use of it. 'Do I perform better by doing this?' 'Does it bring about a reduction in costs?' Practice proves that this intellectual exercise, this art of abstracting, does indeed pay off. The Constitution window yields unexpected insights and ideas that stimulate the continuous improvement of the business processes. Investing in the architecture of the enterprise is mainly a collective activity. The architecture is not developed from behind a desk, but by cooperatively developing and exchanging models about the enterprise. As far as the existing organization is concerned, this investment provides the means to investigate, correct and control the coherence and quality of the business in a well directed manner. In this way, developing an appropriate understanding of the constitution of the enterprise provides a starting point for a new view of process management.

Developing and communicating the constitution contributes to the 'self-learning' capacity of the enterprise. Describing functions in the form of a set of interconnected Key Result Areas serves as a means to provide insight in the way an enterprise can realize their goals. It has been proven in practice that working with the Constitution window can lead to the adjustment of the governance structure of the organization. The architecture can result in specifically highlighting the management role of 'process owner', a step forward in organizational maturity.

Who are involved?

Producing and maintaining the Enterprise Architecture and the descriptions of the Key Result Areas are the fundamentals for controlling and improving the processes. In practice, most of the profit and non-profit organizations have defined their processes (via the Correspondence window) and their agreed approach to collaboration and working methods (via the Construction window). The models of the Constitution window are meant for all those people in the company that feel the need to have an understanding of the 'big picture' of the enterprise. It is not a framework that is set in stone, but it is designed to give structure to the daily work and to stimulate continuous improvement. The starting point is formed by the known activities, arranged by the Enterprise Architecture and developed into Key Result Areas. The key is to do one's best to achieve overview and insight, thereby enabling well directed control, monitoring and comparability. What is not the goal, as mentioned before, is documenting the craftsmanship and skills of each individual employee. The professionally mature employee is the starting point. It is not the intention to have every employee perform their tasks whilst carrying around the diagrams of the Key Result Areas. It is however allowed, but only in a metaphorical sense, to carry an awareness of the enterprise as a whole. The stakeholders of the Constitution window are all those employees of the company that should be aware of the architecture and coherence of the enterprise. The Key Result Areas are overview descriptions for the workers ON the quality of the organization. In this way they can be provided with the means to get a firm grip on practically controlling and monitoring the activities within the organization.

The quality of the constitution

It is a misunderstanding that one should 'implement' a constitution. Anyone in a company has more or less a structured view of the essence of the enterprise and carries a kind of 'big picture' in their head, implicitly. The intention of using the view through the Constitution window is to get a more shared, explicit and formal 'big picture'. It forms the 'logic bubble' from which management shape their business, organize, monitor and intervene. The main value of asking for attention to a commonly adopted architecture lies in synchronizing and reinforcing the images that already exist.

The constitution forms the foundation, the reference and the basis of support for further design of the Enterprise Architecture. This is true in both a technical and a social sense. A technically perfect model (compliant with all drawing conventions) is worth nothing if it has no supporters, or when it is not recognized. Looking through the Constitution window, an enterprise is capable of developing a standard that forms the basis of looking at the business and the organization. And, as we know from experience, a standard does not always have to be perfect. The judgment of the quality of the architecture always takes place in a scene of tension between content and acknowledgement. An architecture sometimes suffers from a lack of purity in the approach of the activities. It remains difficult to completely let go of the organization chart and to focus solely on the activity.

In the case of the car company, theoretically there is only one Key Result Area concerning Sales. From a historical point of view, however, the management of the car company can agree to distinguish two separate Key Result Areas, according to the two historical branches 'Lancia/ Fiat' and 'Mitsubishi/Hyundai'. Such a concession to the purity of the method would perhaps improve the acceptance and the recognisability.

With the constitution, it is feasible to develop the 'logic bubble' of everyone involved with the quality of the organization towards a transferable and shared 'big picture'. It does not matter if this is, for example, an employee who has been tasked to investigate the robustness of the financial decision-making and reporting, or a quality or environmental expert, or an ICT project manager who is involved with automation of some parts of the business. All of these have to be able to work with the model, as if it was a map in which they could record their own assignment or ambitions. The relationship between the various Key Result Areas and their own assignments should be modelled with it, so they can be seen in relation to all the other actual issues that are going on. Via the picture of a key result area, the different 'workers on the quality of the organization' can get sight on their different or even conflicting interests. The Key result Areas are a kind of arena for balancing their interests!

An architecture of the enterprise is not intended for operational use. So a diagram of it should not frustrate a professionally mature employee. An activity diagram that's pointing out the substituent activities and interconnections of a Key Result Area is intended to prescribe a working method. Modern methods of analysis too often concentrate on the work that has to be done and not on the supply of information for control, coordination and accountability associated with this work. It is too easy to prescribe what employees should do and forget that the professionals amongst them have know for a long time what the best approach is. Instead, it is better to concentrate on the information channels and the documents; the messages with which the employees need to perform their activities properly. As mentioned, activities are preferably seen as 'black boxes', containers of craftsmanship and, in this way, they are viewed as 'black boxes' of which it would (in a certain context) be wise to develop agreements on the subject of the actual work (see from chapter 5 onwards).

The Constitution focuses on results. A description of a Key Result Area documents all messages that represent either the control or the accounting of the result(s) of the processes. Regardless of how the work will be performed, the messaging will always have to take place. The messaging is 'abstract' but still 'tangible'. Messages can always be verified because of the unique character of every action and every event in the business. This is the reason why we like to regard messages as being the bridge from the abstract model to the fully implemented and deployed organization.

In the car company, no repair will take place in exactly the way that may have been devised. The only thing to be sure of is that there is a work order that will at a certain moment be followed by a repair report. This repair report explains the way in which the repair was carried out and why it might have differed from the way it was planned.

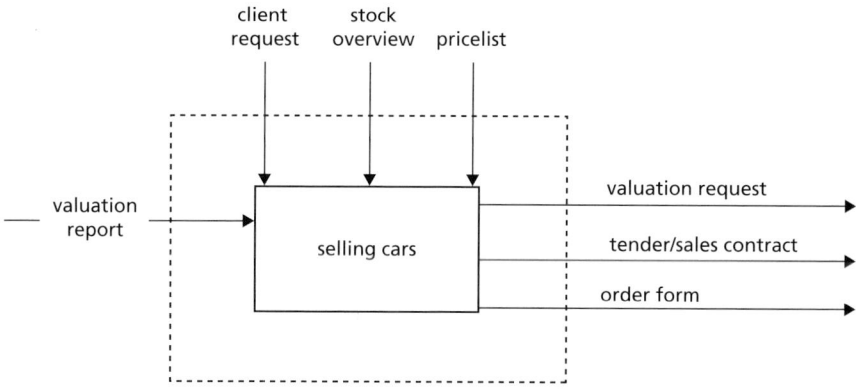

Example 4.   Defining the Key Result Area 'selling cars'.

Working out the diagrams
The development of a first draft of the Enterprise Architecture is the usual way to start mapping the constitution. By means of interviews, brainstorms or discussions it becomes obvious which Key Result Areas are perceived as the most important ones. Picture this information in an 'initial diagram' like in example 1. This primary picture forms the 0.1 version of the Enterprise Architecture. The Key Result Areas mentioned in this version form the guideline to compose the working groups that will provide depth to the Enterprise Architecture by describing the constituent functions. As soon as these working groups are drawing up the Key Result Area descriptions, the understanding of the enterprise is increasing. In the process of drawing up a Key Result Area description and the diagrams that map their coherence, the perceived or aspired Enterprise Architecture is readjusted and the differences incorporated.

Carefully select the people with whom the Key Result Area descriptions are worked out. Is it about analysing a part of the Enterprise Architecture in a small committee? Or is it just making decisions and harmonizing the perception of the Enterprise Architecture? A lot of communication afterwards is avoided by involving the right people. However, gathering too many people can cause serious delays in the overall activity. A group of about six persons is the optimum, combined with clear agreements on how discussions are led and which form of decision-making will be used. Are decisions made by consent (no main principle objections) or by consensus (full concurrence with the risk of compromising)? Always agree in advance how much time the group thinks they need to produce a good diagram. Adhere to this limit rigidly. In spite of the fact that the diagram technique leads to 'converging discussions', it can happen that discussions about Key Result Areas drift on without this leading to a significant increase of the quality of the diagrams.

It is important to lay down the scope of a particular Key Result Area at the start of developing the activity diagram. This leads to a diagram as presented in example 4.

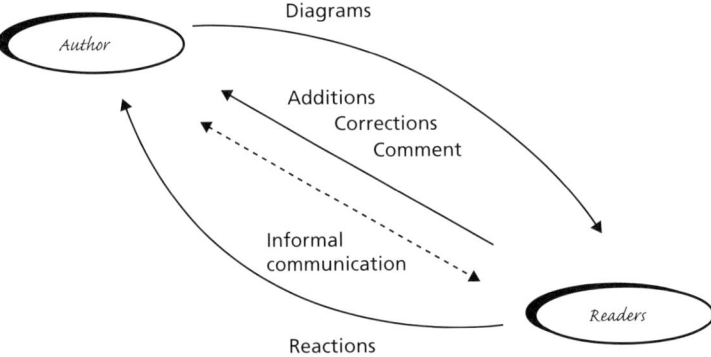

Figure 4.5   The Reader-Author Cycle

By means of a brainstorm, an initial description can be drawn up of the content of the 'box within its bounds'. This brainstorm has to produce two lists. Firstly an overview of all imaginable verbs, the activities that fall within the scope of the diagram, and secondly a list summing up all nouns, the messages that play a role in the execution of the selected part of the business. Subsequently, the brainstorm can be refined with a selection of verbs and nouns that together represent something meaningful.

This selection forms the basis for setting up the Key Result Area description. Arranging, sorting and positioning the verbs and the nouns in boxes and arrows in their coherence will form the first draft of the Key Result Area description. When the members of the working group are sketching and developing the Key Result Area, the conception of the organization as a whole and its constitution become increasingly clear. Often, the arrows or boxes are renamed, arrows get rubbed out, and boxes are moved, united or split in two.

When sketching the first draft, this to and fro communication is an important reason to make the model as complete as possible, including the thoughts and ideas of the members of the working group. E.g. we feel the need to draw in an arrow without being sure whether it should be present in the diagram or not. When we leave this arrow out, we run the risk of forgetting something. The reader can not 'read' this. We had better include the arrow and ask the reader if it is appropriate.

An interaction like this can be achieved by organizing a 'reader-author cycle': a controlled distribution and revision of the Enterprise Architecture and the accompanying descriptions of the building blocks in Key Result Areas.

Prevent the endless circulation or e-mailing of concepts and approved descriptions by making clear agreements in advance. Discuss comments verbally if possible, reach agreements and set them out as drafts. Usually, these agreements are of greater importance than a lengthy e-mail exchange about diagrams.

How far to go on breaking open and getting into more detail?
A Key Result Area can not be broken up when the individual boxes are impossible to split up into further boxes and arrows. The box 'executing repairs' from example 2 is not worked out into more detail because the car company has not agreed on any obligatory messaging between 'working order' and 'repair report'. It is regarded as a 'one undividable container of craftsmanship'; from the perspective of this window it is a black box. In other words, one can state that the Key Result Area description can be viewed as an inventory of the most important communication actions, the interactions between professionals that determine the quality of the operation.

However, the process 'performing repair' can be further divided into activities. This can be made clear by means of a process-flow diagram that forms part of the Correspondence window. How process descriptions are developed and how they, in their turn, form a check upon the completeness and consistency of the described 'mother Key Result Area', is described in chapter 7.

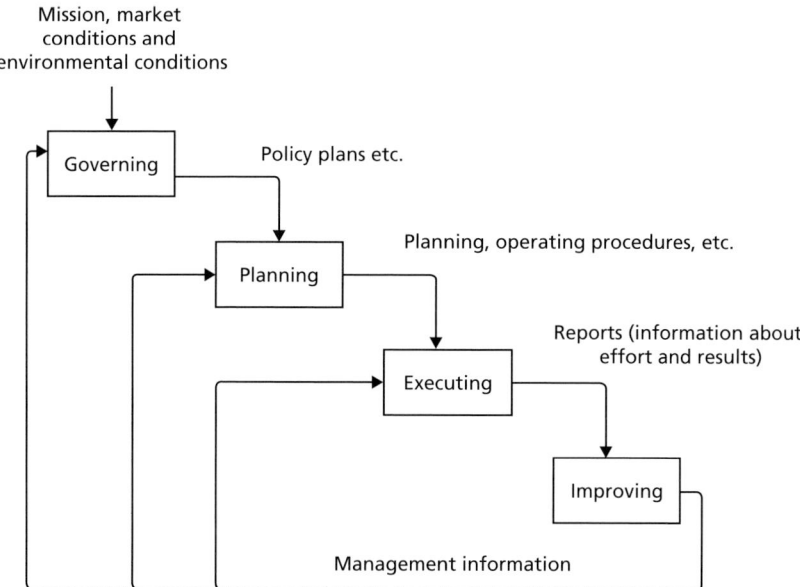

Figure 4.6   Basic model for arranging activities

It is sensible to agree upon a maximum time to be spent on describing the Key Result Areas, for example two half working days with a working group of six people. After this investment the resultant Key Result Areas have to be judged and the working group can compose a 'final' version. In this window, 'final' is relative, because the constitution remains under the influence of new insights in business. It will, particularly in the initial period, be regularly reviewed. This requires as basic premise of 'good enough will do'.

4.5   Reference Model for the enterprise

Developing the Enterprise Architecture can be done using a reference model. With this reference model as a starting point, the activities necessary for guiding, developing, operating and maintaining the business are shown in a coherent manner. Groups of closely connected activities can be sub-divided, for example those concerned with governing the enterprise, planning the business, controlling the primary processes and improving the organization. This division into main groups is also based upon the differences of, for example, the dynamics between various activities belonging to a main group and the corresponding levels of decision: ranging from strategic to tactical to operational. The last main group, 'improving', provides the feedback to and between these different levels (see figure 4.6).

Practice proves that the patterns above can be found in any company, regardless whether it is a veterinary clinic, or a large enterprise in chemicals or the IT sector. In fact, one can talk of a universally applicable structure. This means that some kind of a generic 'template' exists for the Enterprise Architecture. Within a company, such a model can, for instance, be used as a start to monitor and control different business units in the same way. Also, a model such as this can be used within branches or related industries as a common framework, as a reference model for mapping the Enterprise Architecture. At this level of ordering, there is a proven point of departure for developing the Enterprise Architecture. The activities concerned will be clarified later.

Governing the enterprise
This main group includes the management activities but also the control measures that apply as a condition for an effective and efficient organization. One can think of the management of personnel, like recruitment, education and training of employees, the control of the information infrastructure and other means. Think also of activities such as facilities management, finance, automation and office accommodation. Usually these activities are referred to as supportive processes.

Planning the business
The activities in the main group 'planning' are focused upon 'securing' the actual production or service. The primary effect of uncertainty is that it limits an enterprise in terms of how they are able to plan in advance or to decide on activities before they are executed. The arrangements and agreements made as a result of planning form the basis for management of the operational activities. Planning also covers the activities around the receipt and transfer of customer demands and assignments, the design and development of services or products, the planning of operations, and the planning of materials and resources.

Controlling the primary processes
This main group includes the operational activities of the enterprise that in a direct sense add

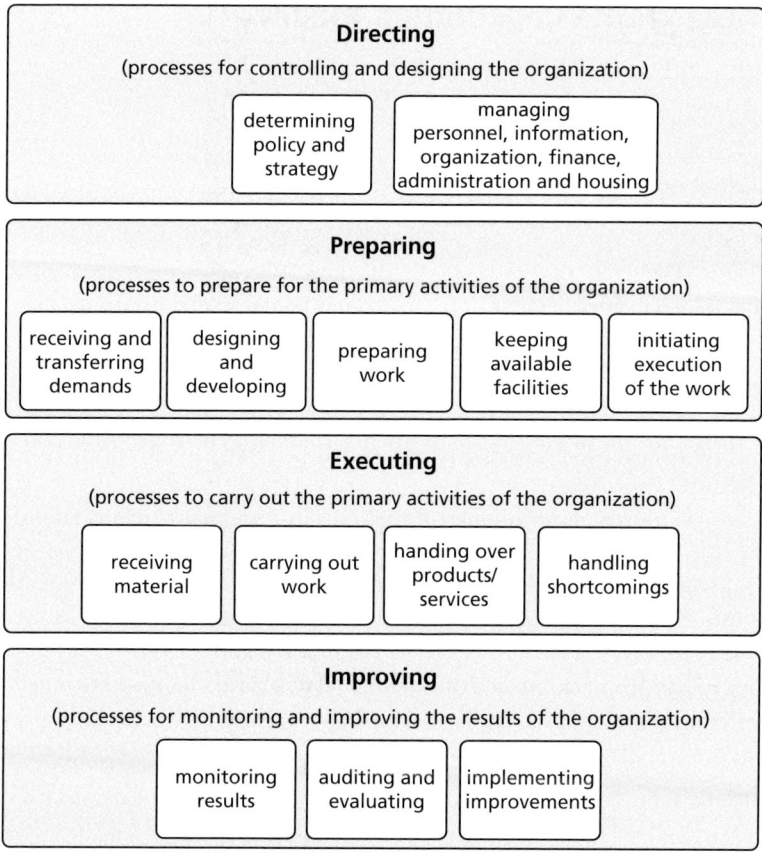

Example 5.   Basic model for arranging activities.

value to the finished product. It encompasses those activities that directly deal with providing services and/or making products. This group also includes logistics and the activities associated with handling defective goods and aftersales service.

Improving the organization
Improving is about taking care of management information and analyzing it. On basis of this information, necessary improvements are initiated, planned and realized. All activities that are executed with the objective of increasing safety, reducing costs and making the work easier are allocated to this group. Improving the business process includes activities around performing internal audits and executing projects for achieving improvements.

The start point of undertaking a basic categorization of the main groups of activities provides a checklist for defining and mapping the interconnected Key Result Areas.

4.6   Tips & Tricks for the Constitution window

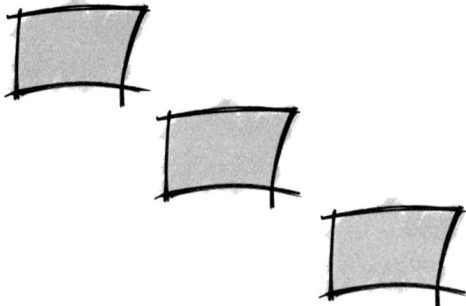

Figure 4.7   Layout of the boxes

Enterprise Architecture

Specific hints and tips that can be helpful when designing the Enterprise Architecture are described below:

- As an option, the Enterprise Architecture can also incorporate important external parties. An Enterprise Architecture incorporating this information can provide a valuable insight into the context of the business.
- By agreeing that Key Result Areas are, like activities and processes, always indicated by a verb, minimizes the chances that the Enterprise Architecture will be confused with the organization chart.

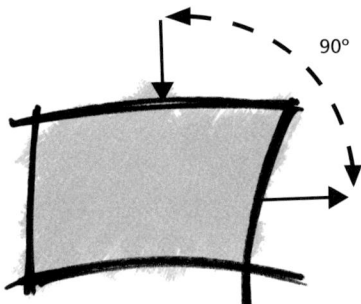

Figure 4.8   Layout of the arrows

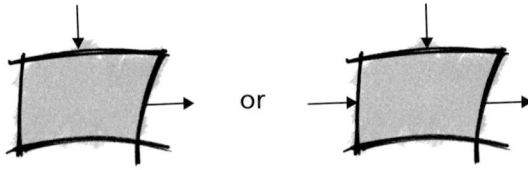

Figure 4.9   Meaning of the arrows

- The boundaries of the Enterprise Architecture often match the boundaries of the company. However, this does not always have to be the case. The Enterprise Architecture can cover just one aspect of the business, for instance facilities management or planning and control.
- The Enterprise Architecture can also be used to provide a view of a specific supply chain.

Think of a number of companies that cooperate closely e.g. as in the automotive industry or the chain of all governmental agencies that are busy with Safety by means of the Criminal Law: the chain of Police Forces, Public Prosecution Offices, Criminal Courts.

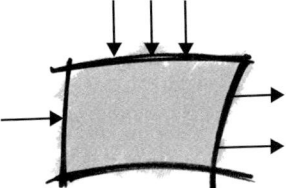

Figure 4.10   Equal distribution of the arrows

Key Result Areas

Diagrams should be kept as simple as possible in order to be clear and easily understood. A number of specific points of guidance are listed below to help archive this:

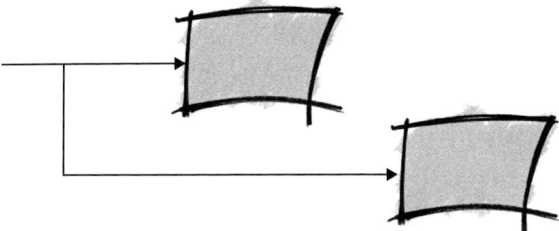

Figure 4.11   Splitting up of arrows

- The use of the Enterprise Architecture and the description of the Key Result Areas is not something that should be undertaken by any employee. Be mindful of the pitfalls of paying too much attention to this diagramming technique, as it is of little use to the average employee. To ensure coherence in the business it is of crucial importance that the employees responsible for this process are completely familiar with the use of this particular window of the SqEME® approach.

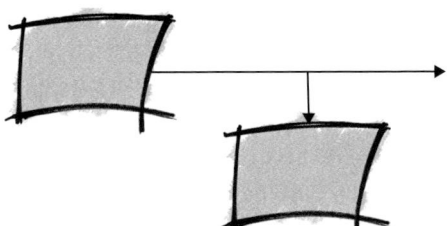

Figure 4.12   Bundling of arrows

- When describing the Key Result Areas, distribute the boxes diagonally from the upper left to the lower right of the diagram. The cascade (waterfall) that is created in this way is ideal for emphasizing dominance, minimizing arrows bends and crossovers, and simplifying feedback.

It is advisable not to draw less than three and not more than five boxes in one diagram. This limitation ensures that models stay legible and can be fully understood and used

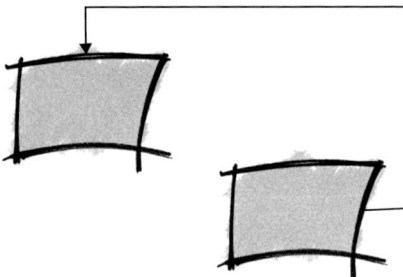

Figure 4.13   Drawing of a control-feedback

- Arrows should touch the boxes at an angle of less than 90 degrees. Draw arrows only horizontally or vertically. This visually makes the boxes stand out as collection points, which is what they are. This rule also makes it easier to follow the direction indicated by the arrows.

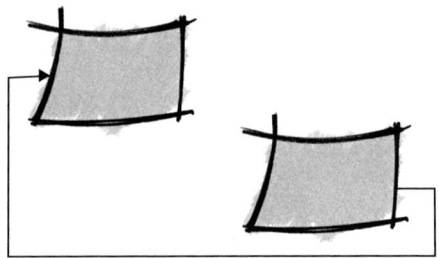

Figure 4.14   Drawing of an input-feedback

- Boxes always have to be provided with one or more control arrows. These arrows initiate and/ or control the execution of the process or tell it what its obligations are. The control arrows form the constraints within which the process takes place. Input arrows, however, are not always required.

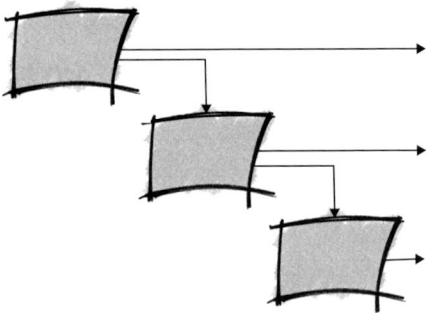

Figure 4.15   Avoiding crossings of arrows

- When a message contains both control information (control) and input information (input), it is drawn just as a control arrow. This reduces the complexity of the diagram and emphasizes the controlling character of the message.
- Allow a reasonable space between the arrows. This provides room for writing in the name. It also helps to distinguish the real number of arrows and simplifies the tracing of their route.

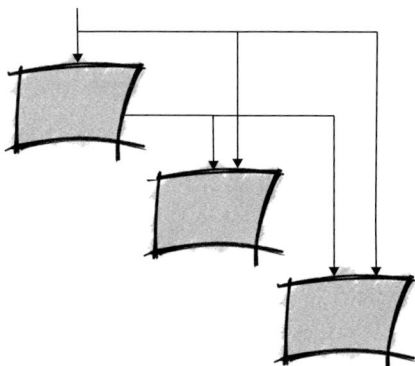

Figure 4.16   Avoiding bends in arrows

- When an arrow has to arrive at more than one box, the arrow should remain as a single line for as long as possible. In this way it is easier to tell that there is only one source for the same message.
- Arrows that have the same source or the same destination when their data is related should be bundled. This will call for a collective (group) name that clarifies the meaning of the data.
- Control-feedback arrows are drawn high up and longitudinally. This shows in a correct way that 'governing' data is fed back and it reduces the crossings of lines to a minimum. It also keeps the control arrows to the upper right part of the diagram.
- Input-feedback arrows are drawn along the bottom of the diagram. This clearly indicates that the data streams are being fed back, and guarantees minimal crossings. It also concentrates input-arrows to the lower left part of the diagram.
- Avoid unnecessary crossings of arrows when they connect to more than one box. This may be the most simple and obvious rule, but it has the largest effect upon the clarity of the diagram.
- Keep the amount of bends and corners in any arrow at a minimum. This rule also reduces the complexity of the diagram.
- The rules for schematically describing Key Result Areas are not complex. Having been shown a good example, many people think they understand what to do. However, an accurate application can be hard to master and requires thorough guidance in the initial phase.
- Numbering Key Result Areas and the underlying activities in a logical way can provide clarity when there are a large amount of building blocks.
- Do not lose too much time debating whether or not a message is controlling. When a message contains information for both governing and accounting purposes it will be drawn as a control message. This reduces complexity and underlines the 'bounding' character of the message.
- In instances where the dominance between two processes is hard to determine, consider simply drawing it with outgoing messages that control in both directions. In this way the negotiation, for example between the making of a 'production plan' and a 'maintenance plan' is clearly shown.

- When mapping the Enterprise Architecture, it should always be clear whether the current practice or the desired situation is intended. In the case of a Key Result Area description, this distinction is often a marginal one. In 90% of the cases, the activities and messages that have been distinguished in a Key Result Area are recognizable in both the current practice and the desired one. The distinction can be found in the agreements about the performance and the appearance of the activities and messages concerned. For instance, one can imagine that when looking through the Construction window, the process 'planning the production' and the message 'production planning' arising out of the decision to change the assignment of duties and the purchase of other planning software are 'stirred up' thoroughly, whilst seen through the Constitution window nothing essential has changed in the enterprise.

4.7   Process Accountability in this window

Looking through the Constitution window, the focus in on questions of a constitutional nature:
- What are the most important Key Result Areas of the enterprise?
- What are the activities and messages within these Key Result Areas?
- What is the formal messaging that exists between the Key Result Areas?

In order to determine and maintain the essential processes and their interdependence it is important that the process accountability is adjusted to reflect the questions related to this window that are mentioned above. A short list of the aspects of process accountability viewed from the perspective of this window are shown below:
- making agreements about the starting points and principles of the enterprise (mission/view/ strategy/policy) and translating them to Key Result Areas;
- explicitly stating the critical results and corresponding messages within the enterprise (the croquet wickets, see also Figure 5.2);
- providing the overview;
- striving to develop the 'big picture' of the enterprise from 'department thinking' to 'process, system and even value chain thinking'.

This list is not complete. In chapter 8 this list will be used to signify process accountability. One of the principles in the SqEME® method is that the aspects mentioned (and others) do not have to be covered by one person. Every individual aspect belonging to this window merits a discussion in order to clarify which person should claim responsibility for the management of such a Key Result Area. This can be the controller, the quality manager, the emergency response officer, the line manager, a member of the management team, etc. Also, for the above mentioned aspects a separate (extra) role can be created, such as that of a process owner or a process manager. The decision on who actually claims responsibility for the different aspects of process management strongly depends of the way processes are governed in the organization.

5 Chemistry

The Chemistry window concentrates upon the 'chemistry' in the community of committed people, the interaction between the professionals in the organization. This 'chemistry' is expressed by studying the information supply, the communication, the incidents of consultation between the professionals who are executing their activities. It is this information supply, the messaging or the conversations between professionals that are essential for the quality of collaboration in the company. This is what aligns the contribution of the individual professionals to the shared ambition of the company.

The Chemistry window answers the question about which interactions and cooperation have been, or should have been, formalized in the organization. By making formal agreements about the information exchange between professionals and using these to formalize the collaboration, a new and powerful dimension is created to influence and control the quality of organizing.

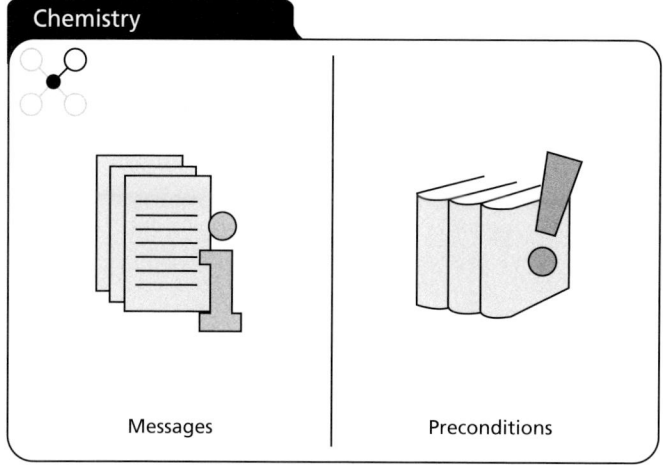

Figure 5.1   The Chemistry window

When carrying out an activity, the quality of information is vital for a successful result. In order to get to grips with the communication that is needed for governing and controlling activities, it is vital to reach agreements about certain issues. An agreement such as this is referred to as a 'message specification' and it is an important instrument for managing the sequential execution of activities. Such chains of successively executed activities are known as processes. The message specification answers the question of which formal agreements have been made that relate to the quality of the cooperation. These message specifications are, so to speak, mini-contracts that set out the agreements on collaboration.

In the example of the car company, it is important that the professionals have the right information at their disposal. Which car is it, what repairs have to be done, what is the origin of the complaint, when should the job be finalized, are there any special work orders of specifications? Without the correct information, the mechanics cannot do their jobs.

And without recording information, the car company as a whole cannot attain its goal. For example, specifying the maintenance activities in the maintenance report is necessary in order to draw up an invoice.

Another important part of the Chemistry window is formed by the preconditions. Through these preconditions the question is answered as to which extra requirements the business should comply with in order to acquire the necessary 'licence to operate'. After all, each company is bound by legislation and regulations. The organization can set itself limits in the way it functions by developing a code of conduct or by developing internal procedures.
This question sits well within the open system thinking that forms the basis of the SqEME® methodology, because effects at the environment level reciprocally influence the functioning of the enterprise itself.

The Chemistry window regards activities as black boxes. The behaviour within the activities is considered by studying the messages 'going in and out'. A message is understood as the representation of a result or event caused by the activity. By establishing agreements about and specifying demands of the information supply, then in fact agreements are made about how employees will collaborate, together with the objectives that are to to be realized By developing an unambiguous view of the Key Result Areas and their interrelations, this window not only maps the most important building blocks, but also makes a statement about the most important 'croquet wickets' of the enterprise (see figure 5.2).

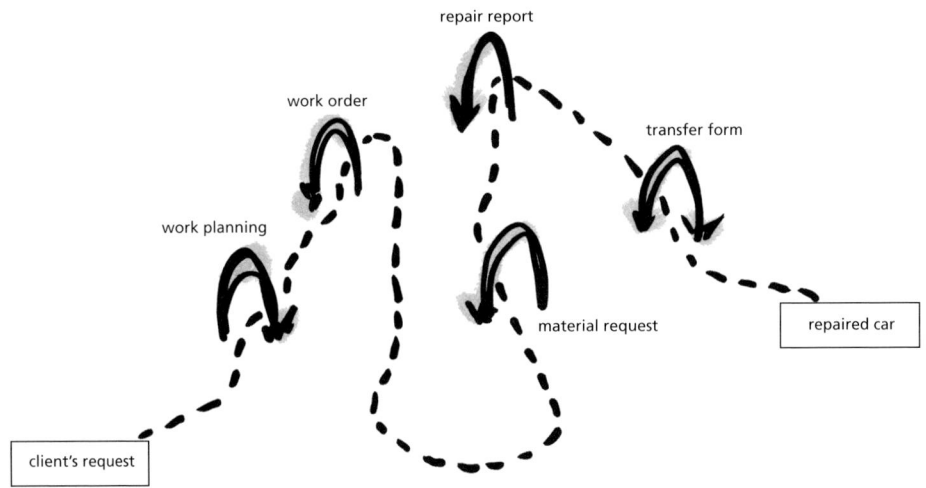

Figure 5.2   Message specifications as croquet wickets in the operation

Language and Signs of this window
The Chemistry window employs the modelling techniques 'message specification' and 'precondition matrix'. For a more detailed description, we refer to section 5.4 (Tips & Tricks) and to Appendix II. There is also a handy pocket guide, called 'Language and Signs'[40], issued by the SqEME® Foundation, that describes all the drawing conventions and supplies tips and examples. Parts of this pocket guide haven been integrated in this chapter.

---

[40] Van Velzen, Van Oosten, Snijders and Hardjono (2007), SqEME® Process Management – Language and Signs.

5.1   Specifying of Messages

Result-oriented professionals mutually commit themselves by drawing up message specifications. In other words: they promise each other to execute their work based on unambiguous acts of communication between themselves. What the commitments actually are, and who is bound to perform accordingly is laid down in detail in the message specifications.

The message specifications that are agreed can be symbolised as the 'croquet wickets' in the descriptions of the Key Result Areas. In order to comply exactly with the client's needs, the ball will have to be driven through the relevant hoops. Even when there is an 'emergency action in between' to help a regular client (repairing a puncture), the messages will have to be completed afterwards. Otherwise warehouse data will be incorrect or no invoice will be sent. When the car company agreed to have a 'work order form' for every activity, this implies that such a form can be retrieved for any client's request that has been actioned. This is in addition to the maintenance report or a repair report and a transfer form.

Information is the means to carry out activities and to undertake them according to the rules that have been agreed upon. This information can be communicated in several ways: by word of mouth, by means of a sticky note, by work order forms, reports, project folders, etc.; with or without the support of ICT. Mapping the messages is about getting an abstract view of the necessary 'chemistry' between professional mature employees. It is an aspect of process accountability in the company. What information transfer should be addressed in order to ensure that the processes are undertaken in the correct way?

The exact manner in which this transfer of messages takes place in practice plays a minor role in the message specification. This question is not less relevant or complex but it is one that has nothing to do with the necessity of an unambiguous information exchange! This is highly related to the statement that can sometimes be heard in business automation: 'Automating a ramshackle organization just provides an automated ramshackle organization.'

A message specification contains some regular items. Below, the items present in a message specification are summarized and explained.

Name of the message
Every message specification has a unique name. Usually this name is related to the way in which this information transfer can be recognized within the present organization. For example: purchase order, policy plan, repair report, order form, assembly plan, work order etc. It can also be a name for a group of similar messages.

The specified message 'maintenance report' represents a collection of different types of reports. Think of the reports produced after different kinds of major or minor services, the MOT-inspection, the winter check, the summer holiday check, a purchase test and so on. The essence of these messages however is the same, so they can all be described in one specification with the collective noun 'maintenance report'.

Message Specification

Name of message:
Sales contract

The result the message is about:
The purchase/sale of the car has been agreed

Minimal content:
- Identification sales contract (order number/date)
- Name, address, place of residence of buyer
- Sold:
    o Make, type, model, licence nr. colour
    o Accessories / extras
    o Delivery date
    o Selling price (net amount, tax and VAT)
- Purchased (if applicable):
    o Make, type, model, licence nr. colour, mileage
    o Reference to valuation report
    o Selling price (net amount, tax and VAT)
- Special activities
- Applicable delivery conditions
- Signature client

Remarks:
-

Document control:
Period of archiving 11 years.

Preconditions:
-

Resources:
Form Sales Report 16B

People:
1. Draft: Salesman
2. Check: -
3. Authorize: Manager
4. Take action: Salesman
5. Archive: Receptionist

Example 6.   Message specification 'sales contract'.

Result the message is about

Under this heading, the situation communicated by the message is described as precisely as possible. The situation is, of course, the result of the execution of the activity, which this message is the output of. Here, one has to avoid describing an activity. It can be useful to have the description of the situation (in mind) start with the words: 'To achieve that…'

Examples with respect to the car company:
- Purchase order: The order has been placed. (To achieve that the order is placed.)
- Work order: The order to execute the work is given. (To achieve that it has been announced which maintenance/repair work has to be performed within which period of time.)
- Repair report: The repairs have been performed. (To achieve that it is specified which repairs have been carried out.) .

The minimal content of the message

This is a summary of the minimal data elements that the message should contain. What this minimum is, is determined by the information needs of the professional mature employees executing the 'client-activity'. Consider this summary of data elements as the 'obligatory fields' of a form, as found on the internet or in a tax declaration. The message is only valid and useful if this data is present. By collecting this minimal content, an important anchor is created for the data model of the enterprise. This basis is made from a social system perspective. By putting in information architects and information analysts, a link can be made to the ICT architecture of the enterprise. For more information see section 5.3.

Remarks

Under 'remarks', details or peculiarities of the message are mentioned, like its use in specific situations, the frequency and the moment in time at which the message should be either available or that it should have been sent. Under the heading 'remarks' on the message specification, 'work order' logistic instructions can be presented detailing the time at which these orders should be available. For example: available at the latest at 15.00 on the day before the execution of the work order. These kind of remarks can also be structured as 'business rules'.

Document control

In this 'section' all agreements on availability, validity and traceability of the message are specified. Aspects that are significant in this section are, for example, the term of archiving, the means of distribution, the version management and the retrievability of backups. Also, data security issues and measures on the subject of privacy regulations can be mentioned here.

Source and destination of the message

It is indicated which activities are the source and which are the destination of the message. Possible external parties that are destinations for a message can also be mentioned.
Messages coming from the 'outside world', an external party, are mapped as a part of a Key Result Area, but usually it makes no sense to create a message specification for them. After all, their creation takes place outside the sphere of influence of the employee(s) responsible for the process. They come from 'outside', from parties in the environment of the organization. Generally, they have to be accepted as they are.

In the example of the car company, the technical specifications are documentation supplied by the dealer organization. For the car company, the way in which this information is supplied is a fact and cannot be changed.

When the SqEME® methodology is to be used for managing value chains that encompass different autonomous companies, messages that originate externally should be handled differently. In this case, process owners within the internal organization and those of the business partners cooperate to agree upon a message specification that suits the business partners in the whole value chain. It is advisable to indicate which information the internal organization minimally requires to ensure that the processes work correctly throughout the whole value chain.
Practical examples of this are suppliers who manage their logistics in such a way that best suits the material handling of their customers.

5.2   Taking into Account the Preconditions

The preconditions represent the requirements from the general business environment that need to be fulfilled by businesses of all types. These requirements can be in the form of the ISO standards, branch guidelines (HACCP, GxP, etc.), requirements in the area of social entrepreneurship (AA1000, OECD guidelines), or requirements made by legislation. They are the preconditions that the organization has to comply with in order to gain access to the market. It obliges an enterprise to be able to produce objective evidence for the inspectors or auditors of these requirements. In this, one can think of governments, authorities, branch organizations, clients or certifying and inspecting bodies operating on behalf of these parties. In larger organizations where, for example, (internal) corporate guidelines can apply, these requirements can also be categorized as preconditions. This ensures that any independent organizational unit involved works within the preconditions that the company specifies.

The revision in the ISO 9000 series that was introduced in 2000, aligns with the way in which the SqEME® methodology handles the phenomenon of 'preconditions'.

The relationship with the ISO 9000:2000 standard family becomes obvious when we look at the picture in figure 5.3, presenting the process-driven thinking according to ISO. The figure comes from the NEN-EN-ISO 9004:2000 and the NEN-EN-ISO 9001:2000 and shows that the design of the Enterprise Architecture should be more process-driven and less oriented on the elements of the standard. Requirements and guidelines on procedures, coming from earlier ISO standards, have become requirements and guidelines on processes and results. The feedback from the client has become the main driver for the quality of organizing. The idea is that organizations that produce 'concrete life jackets' can meet all requirements but not the ISO standard, because feedback from the client does not influence the way the organization is designed (i.e. how procedures are being set up).

Compliance with preconditions and having sufficient evidence is one aspect of process accountability in the organization. Preconditions that are applicable to a certain result can be mapped per message specification. In this way one can check whether the content of the message actually shows if the preconditions are met. If the message does not demonstrate this, it can mean one of two things. Either the organization does not meet the requirements, or the message lacks

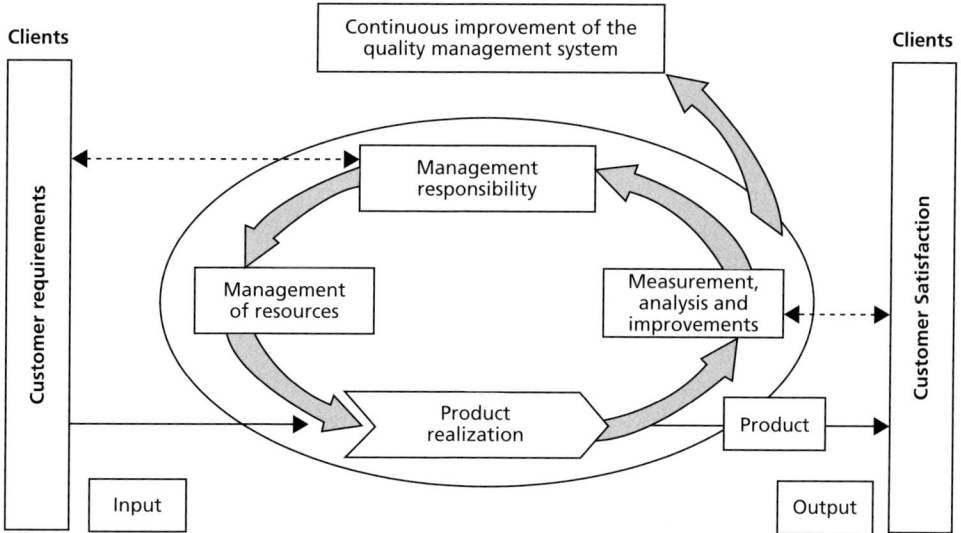

Figure 5.3   Model of a quality management system based upon processes (copied from NEN-EN-ISO 9001:2000)

quality. In the first case an adaptation of the operation is required. In the second case the minimal content of the message concerned has to be adjusted to meet the requirement of transparency (a bureaucratic measure).

In the example of the car company, the periodic checking and calibration of the measuring equipment can be proven by presentation of calibration plans and reports. These messages form the basis of a firm trust in the professionalism of the organization. They are points of attention in the judgement of the dealer organization.

Matrix for verification
A matrix can be used to provide a handy overview of the relationships between the individual requirements and the messages that exist in the different descriptions of the Key Result Areas. Example 7 shows a matrix for a part of the NEN-EN-ISO 9001:2000 in relation to the message specifications in the car company.
In this way the SqEME® methodology offers a practical overview to judge whether the design of the Enterprise Architecture meets the accepted preconditions, and illustrates in detail how the relevant message is translated in response to the specific measures incorporated within the Enterprise Architecture.

From the perspective of information technology, preconditions are also regarded as 'business rules'. It is important to conclude that we are talking about precondition from the perspective of the organization. This means the requirements are defined by the outside world. Preconditions from ICT perspective, the business rules, can principally be written down in the message specification as additional remarks.

Improvement Proposal	Training registration	Training Plan	Management review	Supplier appraisal	Complaint form	Contract appraisal	Order form	Policy plan	Audit report	Audit planning	Messages / NEN-EN-ISO 9001:2000
											4 Quality Management System
											4.1 General Requirements
											4.2 Documentation Requirements
											5 Management Responsibility
											5.1 Management Commitment
											5.2 Customer Focus
								X			5.3 Quality Policy
											5.4 Planning
											5.5 Responsibility, Authority and Communication
			X								5.6 Management Review
											6 Resource Management
											6.1 Provision of Resources
	X	X									6.2 Human Resources
											6.3 Infrastructure
											6.4 Work Environment
											7 Product Realization
											7.1 Planning of Product Realization
						X					7.2 Customer-related Processes
											7.3 Design and Development
				X			X				7.4 Purchasing
											7.5 Production and Service Provision
											7.6 Control of Monitoring and Measuring Devices
											8 Measurement, Analysis and Improvement
											8.1 General
									X	X	8.2 Monitoring and Measuring
											8.3 Control of Nonconformity
											8.4 Analysis of Data
X					X						8.5 Improvement

Example 7.   Matrix messages versus preconditions in the car company.

5.3 Universal Data Element Framework (UDEF)

Nowadays, organizations employ vast amounts of information in many different forms. The more information that is used and stored, the more difficult it becomes to retrieve the information one needs. Defining the message specification in fact determines which information is used in which form.

This is especially the case in the content of the message specification, where it is laid down which data elements the message should ultimately contain. In practice, these data fields are often given different names by different users, with the result that the same data appears repetitively under various names in the message specifications.

For example we have observed more than once that 'client details' are included as a part of the content of a message specification. In other message specifications within the same organization, we found comparable data like 'debtor details' and 'contact details'. Often the same data is meant. When this is true, it is interesting to look at the name and content more closely, e.g. for data like name, address, postal code and place.

Often there is a mismatch at the detail level. In order to match the content of messages properly (both inside and between organizations) one can use a standardized framework of terms. The advantage is that there is a better understanding of the data that is part of one or more messages. Also, based on message specifications, it is easier for information analysts to unravel how messages fit into the information architecture of their own and/or partner organization.

The Universal Data Element Framework (UDEF)[41] is a standardized way to index structured information. The Open Group[42] has developed UDEF with an enthusiastic working group of software suppliers and users to reinforce the interoperability within the internal organization and between organizations. Organizations can employ UDEF to name data. In this way developers of information systems can retrieve and use the desired information more easily. This saves cost in developing computer applications and ICT services.

UDEF is a standard and it can therefore reduce costs within an individual organization as well as between organizations. Large organizations can use UDEF to index their information to easily locate and exchange data between systems. This will mainly lead to a substantial reduction in the costs of programming. For small organizations, the added value will primarily appear in the costs of connecting to an information exchange with large organizations that already use UDEF-enabled software.

On the subject of messaging, UDEF is helpful for specifying content in a standardized manner. Normalizing data is a recognised tool in designing databases. Filing repetitive data in a relational database not only avoids double storage of data, but can also prevent wrong duplicates. Currently, more and more information is exchanged, so the interoperability of data becomes increasingly critical. This is an important reason why the semantics of the content should be taken into

---

[41] For additional info refer to: http://www.opengroup.org/udefinfo/
[42] www.opengroup.org

account when working out messages. Information analysts and software developers can realize the required information exchange in and between organizations both faster and more efficiently.

5.4   Tips & Tricks for the Chemistry window

Message specifications

Message specifications describe the agreements made on the subject of communication in the organization. The following rules help to describe the essential information in the correct place:

- Give message specifications a clear name by which the message is recognized throughout the whole organization. Names like 'plan', 'report' or 'information' are too general. It is better to use 'production plan', 'environment audit report', etc.
- Avoid numbers and/or codes in the name of the message specification. Stated simply, keep identification and codification apart. Numbers and/or codes can be handy to classify and retrieve things during the initial phase. Sooner or later these numbers and/or codes lead to problems because changes are made to the initial principles and/or the categorization, making the numbering and coding incorrect, thus leading to lack of clarity. The alterations make the logic disappear. When computer programmes are employed, it is often possible to generate an index from the programme that matches the classification used at that particular time. This makes it less relevant whether or not numbers are used in names.
- One message specification can describe a family of messages. Both the appearance and application of the individual messages can differ, but then the results to be achieved are identical.
- The specific results of a process are not reflected through the use of a message specification. In the example of the car company, the car to be repaired is not described at all. What is specified is the 'work order' by which the defect of the car or the work to be done is laid down as a representation of the car that needs to be repaired.
- Ensure that a result is not described as an activity in a message specification. This forms an unnecessary and confusing duplication with the process description of which the message concerned is a result. It is wise to have the description of the result beginning with the words 'To achieve that…'.
- By using the opportunities presented by an intranet and internet techniques, an organization is able to implement the agreements on document control very pragmatically. Some organizations have specialists engaged with the intranet and other aspects of documentation concerned with information supply.
- In process or Key Result Area descriptions, the origin and the destination of a message can be retrieved. Messages coming from 'the outside world' do not always have (complete) message specifications included. Messages from external sources are usually things that 'happen' to the organization. Agreements about document control then become important. If there are already agreements or they can established, then message specifications can be applied to 'streamline' the information supply between supply chain partners.
- A good use of document control combined with the person responsible being a good archivist can help to comply with the legislation on archiving *(Public Records Act)* or other archiving requirements.
- Applying the message specification for deployment has similarities to the use of a 'Document Structure Plan' at the same time. Some organizations are legally obliged to have such a DSP-plan.

Preconditions

Some points of attention for the purpose of working out the applicable preconditions are given below.

- One precondition can establish the requirements for multiple messages. Also, several preconditions can apply to one message.
- It is sensible to have the names of the preconditions match the original documents. For example 'ISO 9001:2000 par. 8.2.2. Internal Audit'. In this way it remains clear where certain preconditions originate from. Also one can easily check whether a precondition (e.g. ISO 9001) has been completely implemented.
- Break up extensive lists of requirements into recognizable pieces. This prevents the same precondition from being mentioned in many messages, which can lead to a lack of clarity in terms of which specific part is of influence to the message. Do not, for instance, mention the entire ISO-standard as a precondition, but mention instead the specific sections and their titles instead.
- Many people believe that the era of organizations describing their processes according to the categorization of just one standard is history. Applying the SqEME® method enables an organization to combine the quality handbook, the environmental care handbook, the safety handbook etc. into one Enterprise Architecture that really centres around the business and not around the preconditions. Guided by the preconditions/message matrices, the organization can determine which parts of the Enterprise Architecture are important in relation to a specific precondition, and how all preconditions are handled. For supervisors and external auditors, matrices like this are the guide to lead them along the most important aspects of the Enterprise Architecture. The consequence of centralizing the activities instead of the preconditions is that, when the content and the classification of the preconditions are altered for whatever reason, the organization has simply to adjust the specific relationship between the precondition and the business activities (i.e. the matrix). Without this type of structure in place then such a level of change may require many organizations to rewrite an entire handbook.

5.5 Process Accountability in this window

In the Chemistry window of the SqEME® methodology, the key question is which agreements about the minimal supply of information are laid down in message specifications. The messages form the basis for managing the results of the processes and the constituent activities. The necessity to exchange messages comes from the need for information related to the activities. The quality of the controlling input information is of crucial importance for the final result. Irrespective of the nature of the activity, it is the correctness, completeness and timeliness of the communication that are amongst the most important aspects of process accountability. In order to produce and maintain proper agreements on messages, laid down in the message specifications, it is vital to cover as a minimum the following aspects of process accountability in the organization:

- The setting up of agreements on the quality of the information supply.
- The setting up of agreements about demonstrable compliance to preconditions such as the standard series ISO 9001, ISO 14001, ISO 18001, HACCP, SCC, SOX, HKZ, etc.
- Taking care of the comprehension, coherence and interdependence between the various processes.

This list is not complete. In chapter 8 this list will be used to signify process accountability. One of the principles in the SqEME® method is that the aspects mentioned (and others) do not have to be covered by one person. Every individual aspect belonging to this window merits a discussion in order to clarify which functional role in the organization it belongs to(or should belong to). This can be the controller, the quality manager, the emergency response officer, the line manager, a member of the management team, etc. Also, for the above mentioned aspects a separate (extra) role can be created, such as that of a process owner or a process manager. The decision on who actually claims responsibility for the different aspects of process management strongly depends of the way processes are governed in the organization.

6 Construction

Both the Constitution and the Chemistry windows are meant to think in abstract terms, ignoring the aspects of implementation and control. What are the essential activities, the building blocks of the process-driven enterprise, and what are the messages between these building blocks, the adequate connections so that the enterprise as a whole is able to achieve its goals?

The things we see when we look through the Construction window are much more tangible. It is about organizing the enterprise. Through the use of this window, the question is answered of how the statements and concepts on Constitution and Chemistry can be deployed. What is the influence upon the assignment of tasks, responsibilities and authorities to the professionals in the organization? What is the meaning of this for the provision of resources to enable the people to fulfil their role adequately?

The Construction window offers the most tangible view on the enterprise. Where the Constitution window describes the essential but abstract building blocks of the enterprise and the Chemistry window gives an insight into the connections between these building blocks, this window is about deployment and implementation. The arrow in a diagram of a Key Result Area description can, for example, indicate cooperation between two supply chain partners, in which the agreements on this matter are worked out in a message specification. The Construction window makes it clear that this message is sent as in electronic form by e-mail. In today's business environment, ICT services have a dominant influence on how professionals communicate. An agile construction of the organization will, for example, need professionally highly mature employees and a state of the art information technology infrastructure.

Studying and mapping the enterprise while looking through the Constitution and the Chemistry windows is relatively 'safe'. Its main focus is philosophising about the design and characteristics of the Enterprise Architecture. Ultimately, this has resulted in unambiguous decisions for deployment. Starting from the chosen strategy and taking into account the present operation, changes in the approach to cooperation are either agreed upon or confirmed. For deployment, the issue is to implement the change that has been devised in daily operation. Who should be informed about the new assignment of roles? What resources, in the sense of tools, documented working methods, training, ICT adaptations etc. have to be provided to implement the new structure?

In the Construction window, process management is about the implementation of working methods. It is about concrete thinking in relation to the 'who' and the 'how' of cooperation. This means the distribution of tasks, responsibilities and authorizations. Distinguishing the people and making choices about the roles they can play. In addition, -and this is the key to this window - adequate arrangements have to be made to support those responsible for carrying out the processes (the professionals) in the best possible way!

The language and signs of this window
The Chemistry window employs the following drawing techniques: 'actors/messages matrix' and 'resources/messages matrix'. For a more detailed description, we refer to section 6.3 (Tips &

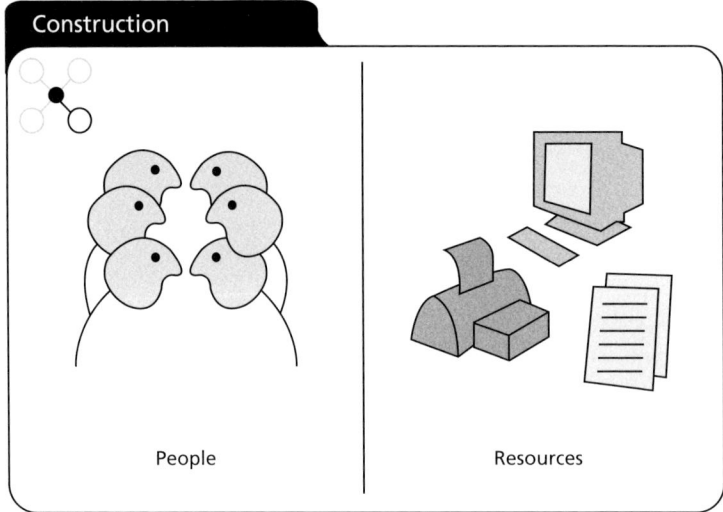

Figure 6.1   The Construction window

Tricks) and to Appendix II. There is also a handy pocket guide, called 'Language and Signs'[43], issued by the SqEME® Foundation, that describes all drawing conventions and supplies tips and examples. Parts of this pocket guide have been integrated in this chapter.

6.1   Types of Actors in an Organization

A company is primarily a community of people. As staff of an organization, these people will, based upon their respective competencies, undertake a range of activities. Often such interrelated activities are clustered into roles or positions that are assigned generally to one ore more employees. Other activities, however, are assigned to individual employees in person, because specific know-how, craftsmanship or experience is required to carry out the activity.

It has proved useful to distinguish some types of 'actors' in an organization. After all, employees can execute their activities as a result of:
• their *position*;
• because they are member of a *board;*
• because they have (temporarily) been charged with a specific *assignment* on the basis of their expertise and skills.

This is how the SqEME® method distinguishes three 'manifestations' of actors:
• Position: a role of an employee for whom the accountability structure has been laid down in an organization chart. Positions are often specified by means of their tasks, responsibilities and authority. Examples of such positions are managing director, purchase manager, product manager, receptionist.
• Board: a group of people who act as a collective and who are authorized to make certain decisions. A characteristic of a board is that the means of decision-making is agreed upon. Examples of a board like this are: management team, project team, Material Review Board.

• Assignment: a person with a specific task, often linked to specialism's or even to formal qualifications. Assignments are delegated to people who, on the basis of special know-how and experience have been (temporarily or permanently) given additional tasks in addition to the regular tasks of their position. Examples of assignments like this include auditor or project manager.

Figure 6.2 shows the various manifestations of actors in the organization and their mutual relationships.

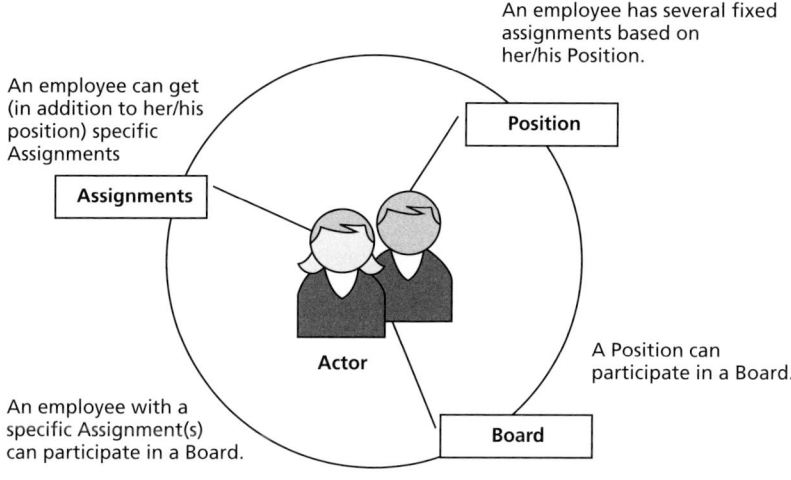

Figure 6.2   The relationships between the different types of the actors

Distribution of powers

Result-oriented management will, of course, hold people responsible for the outcomes of their activities. Whoever adopts this type of management, therefore, commits people to the output of the process. The obligation to 'put in effort' increasingly becomes an obligation to deliver the desired result. A message specification formalizes the commitment of an actor in a particular role with respect to a specific result.

The message specification therefore serves as the handle for employees to arrive at clear agreements about their commitments to deliver specified results. In the example of the car company, the person who formally declares that the car is repaired (and who is entitled to do so according to the appropriate message specification) can be called to account for that. In the first place this actor is held accountable for the repair.

Besides the three 'qualities' of actors, the SqEME® method distinguishes five roles in which the actors can be involved when creating and using messages. These incorporate the administrative roles of 'draft', 'check', 'authorize', 'take action' and 'archive'.

1. Draft

Drafting indicates which actor is entitled to create the message. This actor does not, by definition, have to be responsible for the final result of the message. Whether the actor actually is responsible, depends on the question of whether any other actors have been appointed for checking and / or authorizing the message. A message has at least one entitled author.

2. Check

Checking indicates who is responsible for checking the content of the message, and therefore also the result before it is communicated. If the person responsible for the process deems it necessary, then the checking of messages should be a role that is only be given to actors other than the creator. In such cases the message is concerned with a critical result. Critical in the sense of, for example, safety, risk, the reputation of the enterprise, or financial risk. When it is agreed that such a content-related check by a colleague or an expert is required, it will always take place.

In the car company, for example every repair that has been done is checked and signed off by the workshop manager.

3. Authorize

In authorizing it is determined who is entitled to release the message before it is communicated. This is an authority that can never be delegated to more than one actor under the motto 'you can't have two captains of one ship'. If, for the purposes of authorizing, an actor has been appointed other than the creator, this has to do with policy decisions or decisions with financial implications that exceed the formal authorization of the creator.

In the car company, every purchase order above 25.000 is authorized formally by the board. Only the board has the authorization to sign for amounts as high as this.

Ideally the checking and the authorizing should be done on the authority of the drafter. The starting point is professional maturity. By allocating everything to a single person, the involvement and the accountability of process ownership are stimulated. When employees are empowered to work towards the objectives of the enterprise, when they have been provided with the necessary resources and the skills, and when they have the freedom to make their own decisions, the autonomy of the employee is emphasized and the growth of professional maturity is stimulated. Autonomy does not mean that an employee actually does everything on their own. A professionally mature employee is expected to call in the expertise of others on their own initiative, dependent upon the situation. It is not enforced by management, nor is it embedded in routines. Of course the opposite can also occur. 'Checking' and 'authorizing' can consciously be embedded in a process to control certain risks and to avoid undesirable situations.

4. Take action

To take action indicates who must do something in response to the message. They are the addressees of the message. Who is required to do something with the message? A message requires at least one 'activated person'. If this role is not filled, the message is superfluous and it can obviously be removed from the process and Key Result Area descriptions.

It is the mechanics who have to take action as a result of the work orders. They are the recipients of these messages.

5. Archive

This role indicates the actor who is responsible for carrying out any agreements in relation to keeping the relevant messages available and traceable. This involves the general principles of archiving , including the forms of version administration, the distribution of these messages and the retrievability of backups. Agreements on this are recorded in the message specification under the heading 'document control'.

The roles mentioned above are intended to allocate the responsibilities for the actual creation and usage of messages, and do not include those with respect to the agreement on the message specification itself. It is an aspect of process accountability to draw up message specifications, as well as the documentation in conjunction with the other windows.

Matrix for overview

In the message specification the roles of the people are laid down and assigned to one or more actors in terms of tasks, responsibilities and authorities. After allocating the relevant roles in all message specifications, an overview can be produced in which is clear how each individual is committed to deliver specific results on behalf of the organization. In the Construction window, a matrix is put together that provides a complete overview. A matrix like this presents the roles in relation to the actors and the messages in a neatly arranged and explicit way.

Messages	Actors	Managing Director	Receptionist	Supply manager	Workshop manager	Mechanic		Dealer organization
Delivery report			1.5		2			
Maintenance report			4		5	1.4		
Material request				4.5		1		
Storehouse form				1.4				
Appointment			1		5	4		
Repair report			4		5	1		
Technical specification						4.5		1.3
Work order			1		2.5	4		

(roles)
1. Draft
2. Check
3. Authorize
4. Take action
5. Archive

Example 8.   Matrix messages versus actors of the car company.

Relationships between tasks, responsibilities and authorities

One of the basics of the SqEME® method is the concept of 'self-control'[44]. Essentially, this means that someone is only responsible if a clear assignment (the task) has been given, if the corresponding person has sufficient powers and resources, within acceptable limits, to fulfil their task (authorities) and if this person also can determine at what point they have succeeded in fulfilling their assignment. In this sense the roles of 'draft', 'check' and 'authorize' are clear authorities. The deployment of the organization therefore exists for a large part of delegating authorities.

The way of handling the concepts of tasks, responsibility and authority strongly depends on the dominant management style. It is important that the way in which the roles are distributed appeals to the professional mature employees, and that these people in their turn can be held responsible for the way they handle this in practice. If desired, an organization can retain their own established procedures for the distribution of authority[45], as long as it is defined unambiguously and as long as it achieves the balance between 'control' and 'self-control'.

The TVB session

Since the second half of the eighties, TNO Management Consultants have employed a scientific business administration method for the distribution of authorities that can be usefully used in conjunction with the SqEME® method. It concerns the so-called '*TVB* sessions' *(Taken, Verantwoordelijkheden en Bevoegdheden)* (tasks, responsibilities, authorities), a method which determines who should have the power to make decisions and who should advise upon the major 'areas of accountability'.

During *TVB* sessions, the distribution of powers is discussed in detail and specified in an authority matrix. It is mainly concerned with the tension between 'being allowed to' and 'having to', and between 'freedom' and 'being bound' in the organization (the balance between 'control' and 'self-control'). In *TVB* sessions two types of authorities are distinguished:
- decision authority, symbolized by a 'filled dot';
- advice authority, symbolized by an 'empty dot'.

Figure 6.3 compares the two types of authorities with the roles defined in the SqEME® method. On the basis of the results of a *TVB* session, the assignment of the roles in the messages can be made specific.

Phase	Roles according to SqEME®	Types of authority according to *TVB* Session
Making decisions	Draft	○
	Check	○
	Authorize	●
Following up of making decisions	Take action	●
	Archive	○

Figure 6.3   Roles according to SqEME® and types of authorities according to TVB sessions

---

[44] Juran (1988), Juran's Quality Control Handbook
[45] Ahaus (1994), *Bevoegdheidsverdeling en organisatie;* Ahaus (2005), *Dialoog over bevoegdheid en verantwoordelijkheid.*

RASCI method

The RASCI method can also be used for the purpose of defining tasks, responsibilities and authorities. The letters of RASCI represent the following roles:

- Responsible: the person responsible for the result.
- Accountable: the person who is entitled to call the process owner to account regarding the result.
- Supportive: the people who are productive, those who help the process owner in achieving the result.
- Consulted: the ones who are consulted for the achievement of the result.
- Informed: the ones who are informed afterwards. They are not able to influence the result at that point.

The involvement of employees in processes is recorded by means of these five roles. These roles can differ per activity. A clear difference is that this method links the roles to the processes/activities, whereas the SqEME® method prefers to links the roles to the results (messages).

6.2 Providing resources

Resources are the means (obligatory or not) by which the person responsible for the process provides support to the worker and/or helps them communicate the result of their effort. In organizations a variety of such mechanisms are developed and implemented in order to support a result-oriented operation, guarantee the quality of the work and facilitate the information exchange. The need for these supportive facilities for professionals differs significantly between organizations.

Factors such as the nature of the work, the employment of regular and temporary workers, the requirements for transparency of actions and the risk of the work explain the presence of many or fewer such support mechanisms within an organization. Common resources are templates (standard forms, checklists), ICT services (computer applications), protocols (directives, work instructions) and specific education. As part of process accountability, the means that are put at the disposal of the employees are indicated under the heading of 'resources'. When desired, one can determine whether the use of a specific resource is either obligatory or optional. The means that are provided have to make the realization of the result and the associated communication easier in every respect.

Templates

Templates are the empty documents, the forms that are used to communicate the final result of an activity. A template is filled in during the execution of the activity, forming the final message. Templates can be made available on paper or in electronic form. The basic idea is that by making templates available, people in the organization are more likely to adhere to the standard operating procedures. The desired way of operating becomes engrained as a habit, a daily routine.

In the car company, the agreements on service reports and repair reports are implemented with a whole range of available templates, adjusted to the nature of the work. Think of the form for an MOT check, the forms for the execution of minor and major services for the several types of cars, the checklist for diagnosing technical problems and the carrying out of repairs.

ICT services
The operational activities are supported by ICT services. They replace the vast amount of paper documents and also enable the organization to handle information in a more flexible way and to perform analyses as required. The ICT department assists with the data input, the processing, the transmission and the delivery of the message. Chapter 9 also covers the potential opportunities for ICT to enhance the organization: ICT as an enabler for business excellence!

The message exchange centred around the stock control in the warehouse of the car company is primarily supported by ICT. The car company can also consider whether to replace the planning board – which is filled in and kept up- to-date manually - with an automated planning system. Whether an enhancement like this will be an improvement to the business process strongly depends of the scale and complexity of the work. Choices of this kind can be motivated by the requirement for management information.

Protocols
Protocols define the way in which certain activities should be performed. Other names for this include work instructions, standard operating procedures (SOP's) and checklists. They can be used where desired, or where legally obliged, to supply the professional with detailed information.

The trade-in price is a part of the sales contract. In the car company, the agreed way to calculate the price of the goods and services is worked out by means of a protocol. This protocol is identified as a mechanism within the message specification 'sales contract'.

From process descriptions (see chapter 7), one can also refer to specific protocols. In these cases, the protocols are specified in work instructions. They often explain how certain activities mentioned in the process description have to be carried out.

Education and training
In addition to making available useful resources like those mentioned above, in many cases it is also desirable to provide specific education modules and training for the employees involved.

One can imagine that the car company, or rather the dealer organization, provides education on the subject of 'work preparation' to improve the quality of the 'work orders'.

6.3   Tips & Tricks for the Construction window

People
By explicitly allocating the operational and the process management roles to the relevant messages, a clear picture is created of the collaboration between the people in the organization. Some points of attention are mentioned below that can contribute to a transparent and unambiguous description of these roles:
• Respect the rules mentioned in figure 6.4 to assign employees and their operational role to a message.
• Sometimes a role is linked to a specific individual. In this case it is not possible to mention a position, an assignment or a board. In such a case, don't hesitate to mention the name of the appropriate person.

- Often, job descriptions in which tasks, responsibilities and authorities concerning a specific position in the organization are already documented and available in the organization. Ensure that the assignment of roles matches these job descriptions.

Roles	When to fill in	Number of actors
1. Draft	Always	One or more
2. Check	If necessary	One or more
3. Authorize	If necessary	One
4. Take action	Always	One or more
5. Archive	Always	One

Figure 6.4   Required roles and numbers of actors

- The matrix of tasks, responsibilities and authorities shows the involvement of people in the organization. In this, the focus is on gaining an insight into the agreements about the design and deployment of the business process. However, this matrix does not replace the job descriptions in an organization. The job descriptions often contain more information and will be used for other purposes, like calculating salary or as the basis for an assessment.
- Avoid the use of the formal 'checking' and 'authorizing' of messages as far as possible, since it conflicts with a corporate culture of 'professionally mature employees with a minimum of bureaucracy'.
- As part of the 'taking action' activity, only mention those actors that are required in all cases to act positively upon receipt of the message. In the case of clear and correctly implemented agreements on document control, the routine sending of messages 'for information' can be omitted.
- Unambiguously mapping the document control agreements and clearly appointing a person who is responsible for the archiving leads, in most organizations, to a drastic clear out of both company and personal archives. Frequently, putting in place clear document control agreements can achieve considerable savings, quite apart from the general advantage of having a reliable information supply.

Resources

A brief summary of some key points that provide guidance on the required resources is given below:

- One resource can be used for several messages. In this case, for practical and/or efficiency reasons, just one resource should be implemented to combine the information of several messages. It remains important to specify these messages separately.
- For one message, the provision of more than one resource can be agreed upon. In this case, several means are employed to get to the desired result. It is important to produce one single message specification instead of describing all forms or appearances of the messages. The latter can lead to many similar message specifications.
- 'Separate' electronic documents have to be defined as templates and not as applications. Only when the application is a tool for collecting and processing the data can it be regarded as an application. The tool and the data can not be seen separately. The result is that with an

application, the data is filed in a database. A template just structures the way that the data is filled in.

- Indicate specific training courses only as a resource if an actor has specific qualifications for performing the required role. General education is defined in the list of demands applicable to a position, an assignment, or a board.
- Be careful applying protocols. By defining all sorts of protocols, the situation can arise where too many details have been described. This can lead to unnecessary bureaucracy and it restricts the professional in their actions. It also is expensive to keep all this information up-to-date.
- Applying resources is most efficient if the professionally mature employee really understands the benefits of committing to the desired way of working.
- References to ICT services should be as detailed as possible. This ensures that any changes in message specifications can be implemented in ICT in a well directed manner. Or the other way round, change requests for ICT-services can be assessed on the basis of agreements laid down in the message specifications.
- Provisions can also exist by means of simple signs, notices at machines, stickers, posters etc. They do not, by definition, have to be extensive forms.
- In a matrix, the resources can be listed against, for example, actors and/or messages. In this way, it is clear at first glance the people or messages for which a resource works. This is particularly useful when making decisions about the replacement of such mechanisms and the likely effects of that.

6.4   Process Accountability in this window

In the Construction window of the SqEME® method the focus is upon how the work is actually executed. How are the tasks and powers distributed between the various actors? And which resources have been implemented in the organization to ensure the activities take place in the right way, on the right moment? In short, it looks at deployment.

It is important when implementing processes to assign within the organization the aspects mentioned below, at the very least. In the framework of process management, the deployment issues are the most tangible aspects of process accountability. They are the things that really 'touch' the work of the professionals. They bridge 'working ON the organization' to support 'working IN the organization':

- the distribution of the operational tasks, responsibilities and authorities;
  - distinguishing separate positions, assignments and boards;
  - matching the roles to the existing job descriptions.
- having job performance reviews with employees;
- allocating budgets;
- taking care of education and training of employees;
- taking care of ICT development and implementation, the use of forms, etc.;
- making knowledge tacit in knowledge systems (where necessary);
- providing resources and taking measures that are necessary for the execution and management of the work.

This list is far from complete. In chapter 8 this list is used to further explore and explain the concept of process accountability. A key point of the SqEME® methodology is that the aspects mentioned above should not be covered by only one person. It is worth discussing for every individual aspect which people are committed and who wants to take the lead. This can be the internal controller, the quality manager, the IER officer, the line manager, a member of the MT, etc. Also a separate (extra) role can be created to cover the aspects mentioned above, such as a process coordinator, process owner or process manager. How a role like this is given shape in the framework of process management strongly depends on the way the role is embedded in the governance structure of the enterprise.

7 Correspondence

The Correspondence window is used to get a picture of the dynamics of the enterprise 'in operation'. It is about monitoring the business. Do business processes proceed as visualised and agreed upon and is the performance of these processes according to the objectives? These are two questions about the functioning of the 'operational system' that has been agreed upon.

This window could be addressed with names like 'Control', 'Compliance' or 'Conformity'. However, we have deliberately avoided doing so, because these are all concepts that you can use this window for. For the sake of explaining what SqEME® is about, a more fundamental term has been chosen that makes clear what the essence of looking through this window actually is! This window is about defining the relationship of correspondence[46], providing the means for stating that a proposition corresponds with the facts[47]. In physics, the correspondence principle[48] states that theories must agree with experimental evidence. In quantum mechanics, 'correspondence rules' refer to the principle of replacing physical quantities with operators[49]. Also, in general mathematics, correspondence is an alternative term for a relation between two sets, like different elements or concepts of the business. Of course, for pragmatic reasons, the user of the SqEME® approach for process management can choose, if so desired, to use terms like Control or Compliance to address this window.

Through the Correspondence window, one looks at how the organization performs. The dynamics of the organization are monitored and, if necessary and possible, controlled. This is done by providing an insight into the progress of the processes being undertaken and their respective results. Processes are defined as a collection of successive executed activities, as described in section 4.3 with reference to the relationship between the concepts of Key Result Areas, activities and processes.

The Correspondence window is concerned with questions like: Who does what at which moment? Progress is monitored by means of performance indicators. After all, obtaining management information about the operation is the 'final piece' or 'essential part' of the result-oriented organization.

Looking through the Correspondence window, the business can be viewed by means of process flowcharts and performance indicators. There are many kinds of flowcharts, dependent upon the objective that is required. The descriptions of processes as they relate to this window are aimed at building a bridge between the abstract 'drawings' of the enterprise, as conceived in the Constitution and the Chemistry windows, and the perception of the business, the manifestation of processes by the people in the organization.

---

[46] Wittgenstein, Tractatus Logico-Philosophicus, translated by C.K. Ogden (1922)
[47] Habermas, Jürgen (2003), Truth and Justification, Barbara Fultner (trans.), MIT Press, Cambridge, MA.
[48] the correspondence principle is a quantitative tool in the old quantum theory, explicitly formulated by Niels Bohr in 1923. It says that the behavior of quantum mechanical systems reproduces classical physics in the limit of large quantum numbers.
[49] Carnap, R. (1950) "Empiricism, Semantics, and Ontology," in Moser & Nat, Human Knowledge Oxford Univ. Press. (2003).

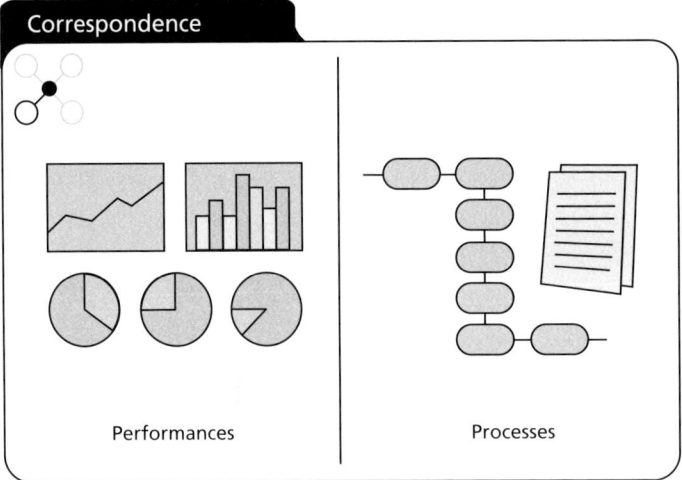

Figure 7.1   The Correspondence window

The sequence of creating, reviewing, using and evaluating process descriptions is eminently suitable to obtaining a view of the differences between the building plan and the building. If differences are found, there is work to do for the process owner. Raising the alarm on the Constitution window means reconsidering the Enterprise Architecture. Putting effort into the Construction window is synonymous with investing in the practical operation.

Performance indicators are the criteria by which one can determine whether the quality of the work undertaken is within the boundaries of acceptability. The performance indicators form the 'cockpit' of the organization. The cockpit presents information on all relevant processes in a balanced manner, so one can respond to an imbalance in the performance of the business process -or a part of it- adequately and in time.

The Correspondence window regards processes as chains of activities that can be managed and controlled by monitoring the process flow. Processes are, as far as is reasonably possible, made predictable and proceed within the agreed boundaries. Deviations with regard to these boundaries must be corrected as soon as possible. Apart from that, the way of handling the performance indicators strongly depends on the dominant management style and corporate culture. Deviations with regard to the working system can also be an important trigger to learn from and adjust the organization in response to possible changes in the surroundings. Having the dynamics in control in this way signifies continuous improvement and adaptation of the operation; adjustment of the course of the process.

The Language and Signs of this window
In the Correspondence window the drawing techniques 'process descriptions' and 'performance indicators' are used. For a more detailed description of the drawing conventions and examples we refer to section 7.3 (Tops & tricks) and appendix 2. There is also a handy pocket guide, called 'Language and Signs'[50], issued by the SqEME® Foundation, that describes all drawing

---

[50] Van Velzen, Van Oosten, Snijders and Hardjono (2007), SqEME® Process Management – Language and Signs.

conventions and provides tips and examples. Parts of this pocket guide haven been integrated in this chapter.

7.1 Describing Processes

The conventions for designing process flowcharts are based on a 'five column' structure. They are designed in a way that enables checking of the abstract interaction diagrams of the Key Result Areas against the background of daily practice and vice versa (!). The process descriptions map which activities take place successively and what role messages play in this. In effect, this 'zooms in' on the specific building blocks of a Key Result Area or the interconnection between those Key Result Areas by means of the workflow. In other words, a close-up view is achieved.

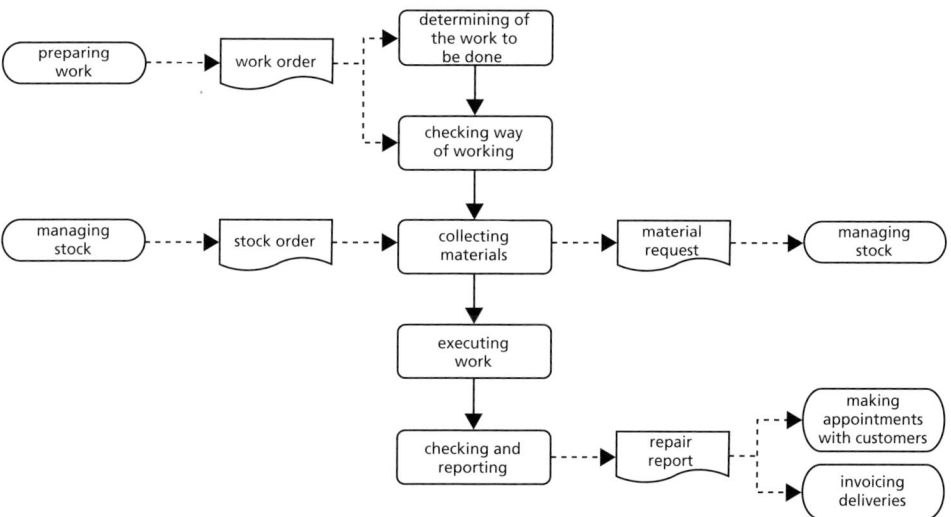

Example 9.   Process description 'executing repairs'.

When developing a process description, the involvement of the workers in the organization is crucial. After all, they represent the 'core competence'; they know better than anybody else what activities are involved, how these activities are (or should be) performed and how the respective activities co-exist. Depending on the approach, they fulfil an active role in describing or reviewing and completing the process descriptions. Although the diagram technique is partially fact (see following chapters), the 'degree of freedom' is much larger when compared to creating a message specification,. The communication between the process owner and the process executors comes first. When considered in this way, creating a process description requires less conformity than describing a Key Result Area and developing a message specification.

The description of 'executing repairs' is not intended to be a work instruction for individual mechanics or the workshop manager. The diagram sketches the steps of the repair process, what information has to be available for the repair process and which messages must be passed on to other processes. With this description it can be explained to anyone in the car company how the activities take place and how they interconnect in the chain of business processes. According to this guideline, the workers in the organization can be questioned about their way of working, information needs and opportunities for improvements.

The process descriptions provide an insight into the routine or sequence of activities within a process, and the information supply that plays a role in this. A process description shows what happens. The key point is that anyone has to be able to read and understand these diagrams easily, without the necessity of training in advance. This is why the SqEME® method decided that process descriptions should consist of a schematic part and a descriptive part. The descriptive part contains a short explanation of the activities shown in the schematic part. Unlike extensive texts, diagrams are clear, comprehensive, easy to communicate, and they can be tested to ensure their consistency and completeness. The schematic part uses symbols as shown in figure 7.2.

Activities
In the diagram, the activities in the process are shown as rectangular shapes [symbols]. The name of every activity is listed in the rectangle and the sequential order is from the top to the bottom.

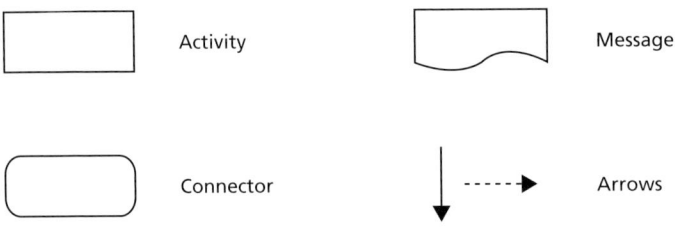

Figure 7.2   The symbols in a process flowchart

For 'insiders' the process is sufficiently clear. For anyone who needs more information about the process, every rectangle comes with a short explanation in a separate frame, describing the activity in more detail. Decision taking that is part of an activity is not drawn explicitly in the diagram; where necessary it is described in the explanatory notes. With regard to the explanation, there is some tension between the familiarity for the employees at one hand and the 'maintainability' of the diagrams at the other. For the benefit of their maintenance, there are restrictions on the explanations that come with each activity. Preferably, the explanation does not mention who performs the activity or how it is executed. The agreements on the 'who' are to be recorded in the message specifications. For agreements on the subject of the 'how', referral is made to specific (separate) instructions or protocols.

Messages
Messages that are of interest to a process are represented by document symbols. The incoming messages, the inputs as well as the controls of the activities in the process, are shown on the left side. The outgoing messages, the outputs of an activity, are shown at the right. The symbol contains the name of the related message. The messages that are shown in the process descriptions have to correspond with the incoming and outgoing arrows around the corresponding activity in the interaction diagram of the related Key Result Area. For all the messages mentioned, a message specification has to be laid down.

Connectors

Connector symbols are linked to the messages. They indicate the supplier processes or client processes of the documents involved. They may also refer to an external entity, not covered by the specific Key Result Area. Through the use of these links, the consistency between process descriptions and Key Result Area descriptions can be ensured.

Arrows

The symbols described above are linked by means of arrows. The links between activities are represented by continuous lines (drawn vertically), stating the time-based sequence of activities. The links between activities on one side and documents and connectors on the other are indicated by interrupted lines (horizontally), stating the flow of information.

Added value of process flowcharts

When studied closely, a process flowchart appears to contain little more information than an interaction diagram describing a Key Result Area. It still is not the intention to describe who performs the work, leaving alone how it is performed. A process flowchart just describes the regular steps in the process, often in a little more detail. These steps are described in just two or three sentences and the relationship between messages and specific activities is mapped in more detail. Then what is the value of a process flowchart?

In the first place, a process flowchart is much easier to explain and discuss than a Key Result Area description because of its greater level of detail. Showing an employee a Key Result Area description and then asking the question 'Is this the way you work?' generally just results in a frown on the face of the employee. However, on the basis of a process flowchart one can immediately -without any further explanation of the drawing technique- have a meaningful dialogue about the method of working. The process flowchart is an easily accessible document, recording the essence of an individual process and the way that it fits into the business process as a whole.

The second and perhaps the most important value cannot be found in the process flowchart itself, but in the process of describing, evaluating and maintaining the process flowchart. The activities carried out for this purpose directly relate to the evolving understanding of the essential business activities and their interrelations. Think of the following scenarios:

• With an abstract interaction diagram of a Key Result Area as a start point, a group of operational experts are asked to describe the processes concerned and to come up with specific suggestions to improve the Enterprise Architecture.

• The twenty most important processes in a company have been identified on basis of the present perception of the Enterprise Architecture. These processes are mapped according to the conventions described above, with the existing working methods as a basis. After this activity the concerning group of people who delivered this 'big picture' really share their view on the enterprise.

• Internal audits are being done, using the process flowcharts as a guideline. These audits are meant to examine whether the actual execution of the business processes diverges from the initial ideas and agreements.

Al these exercises undoubtedly unveil differences between description and reality. After all, in the operation lessons are learnt about the way of working and best practices are developed. It is an aspect of process accountability to decide whether interventions are necessary because of the business processes, the information supply between processes, or in the way in which the principles have been implemented. This means starting an improvement process or putting together an improvement working group.

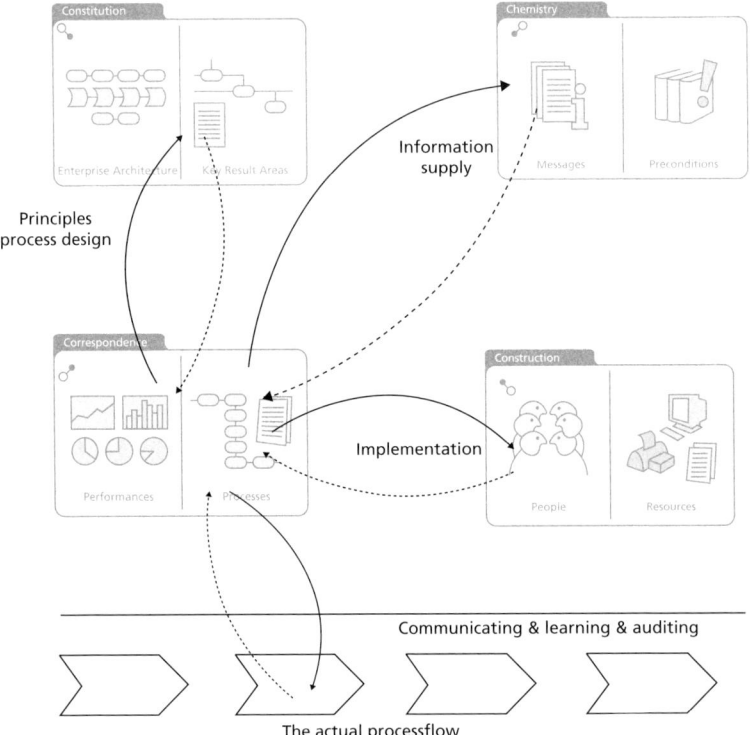

Figure 7.3   Possible interventions by the process owner

Converting existing process flowcharts

Every organization already has process flowcharts, in whatever form. The SqEME® method supplies the handles to restructure the existing description in order to achieve an arrangement that, in general, takes into account the goal, the target group and the maintainability of the descriptions in an improved manner. Therefore, existing descriptions remain of value, but they will be restructured.

Many organizations have documented procedures and work instructions at their disposal. What attracts attention when comparing these documents with the examples shown in the previous chapters is that nearly all the information contained in these documents can be given a place in the four windows of the SqEME® method. In any case, this structure yields the organization a considerable saving of costs in terms of maintaining the documentation. Besides, a transition like this, providing that it is approached as an organizational development and not as a technical project will help the organization in the future with respect to their business structure, their corporate culture and their style of management.

As an illustration, the use of the process flowchart for concluding a contractual deal as a part of selling cars is shown in example 10. For the purpose of testing the consistency of the process flowchart, the relevant part of a Key Result Area interaction diagram is added.

Other techniques for describing processes

Within the scope of this book, process flowcharts have been dealt with on the basis of the standard conventions (Language and Signs) that are the preferred approach in the SqEME® methodology. It is also possible to use other techniques and conventions to map processes. The SqEME® method does not want to stubbornly insist on the use of a particular technique. Whenever an organization uses another technique for describing processes that matches the perception of the employee better, then it is fine to use that. The advantage is that it often better matches practical issues for which the SqEME® method is employed. Some examples of techniques for describing processes at the level of abstraction used in the Correspondence window are 'swimming lanes' and the method of 'Event-driven Process Chain' (EPC).

The express condition is that the techniques of description have to be consistent with the other windows of the SqEME® method. Practice often shows that these description techniques are not one-to-one fits with the other windows of the SqEME®-method, because they have been developed for specific applications. Figure 7.4 shows how the methods mentioned above fit the windows of the SqEME® method.

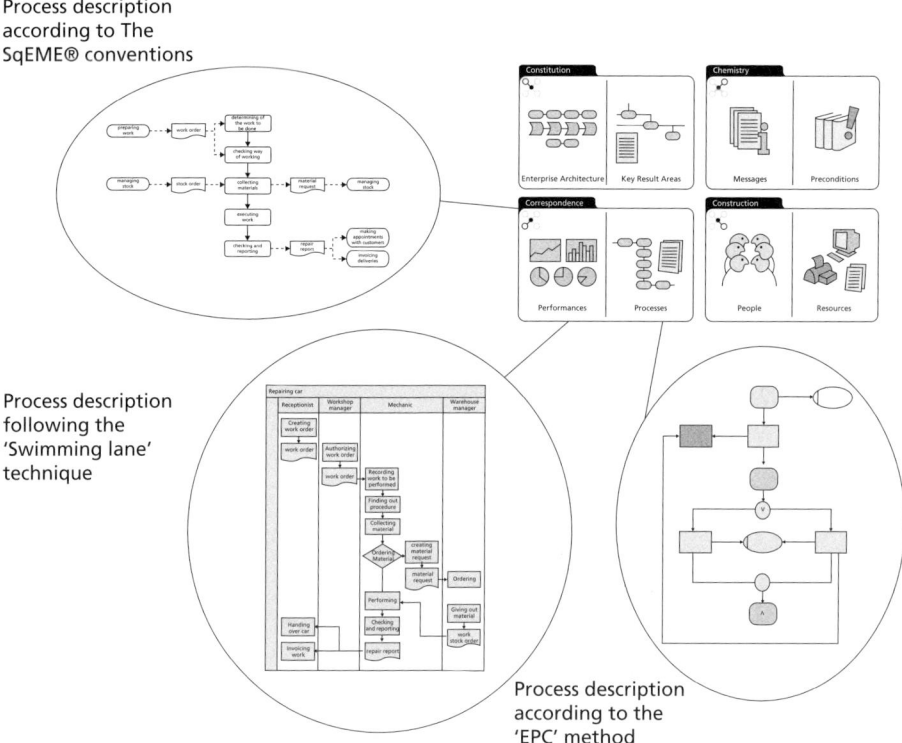

Process description according to The SqEME® conventions

Process description following the 'Swimming lane' technique

Process description according to the 'EPC' method

Figure 7.4   Application of different methods for working out process descriptions

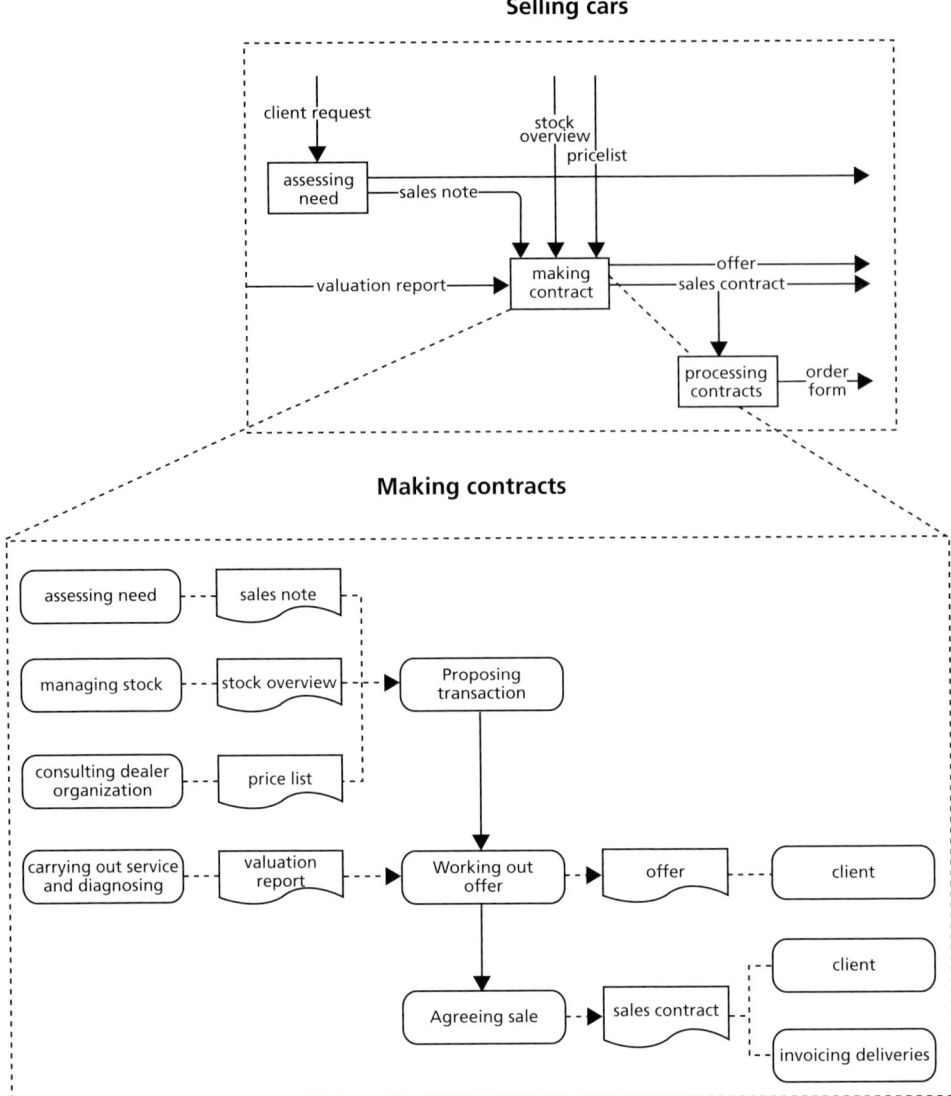

Example 10.   Consistency between Key Result Area and process flowchart.

Swimming lanes

The 'swimming lane' technique in general follows the column structure that is used in the SqEME® method. Yet the 'swimming lane' also displays the course of the process between the actors in the organization. For this purpose, the model is extended by extra columns. The activity is put in the column of the actor who executes it. By joining these activities together, a 'swimming lane' is created, that sequentially shows who does what. As long as the consistency with the Key Result Area interaction diagram is maintained, the 'swimming lane' method can perfectly be applied within the SqEME® method (see example 11).

Event-driven Process Chain (EPC)

An EPC is a sequential representation of events and activities. A set of symbols is used to represent organizational units, supportive systems and decisions (see figure 7.5). EPC enables the course of the process to be modelled in much the same way as the process flowchart of the SqEME® approach. When describing the processes according to the language and signs of the SqEME® approach, some details are consciously left out of the modelled process flowchart; the 'what and how questions' are answered via the models used for the Construction window. This more or less forces the user to concentrate on the activities taking place in the process. When modelling, EPC uses more objects, which means that issues from the Construction window, such as people and resources become visible in the description. Also, the descriptions include more details and the decisions are modelled. Descriptions according to the SqEME®-method see the latter as part of the activities. The result of the decision is presented in the messages that form the output of the activity concerned.

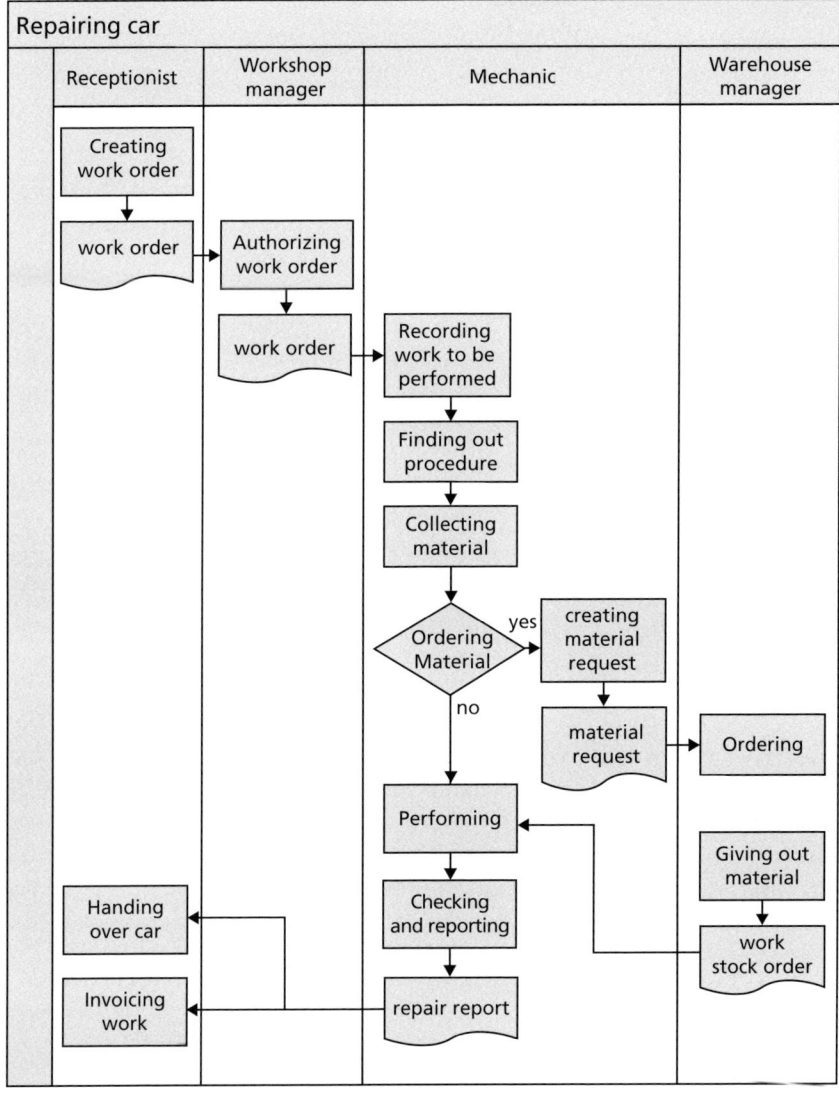

Example 11.   Process description by the 'swimming lane' methodology.

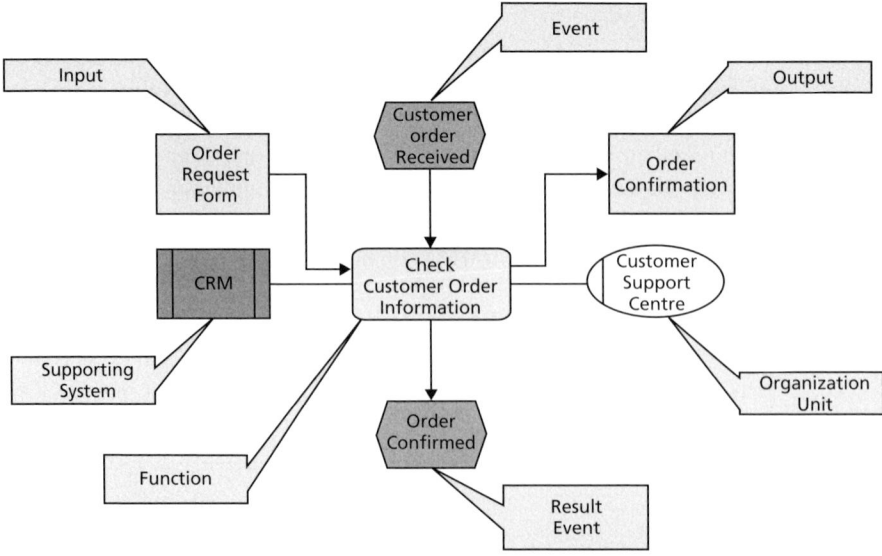

Figure 7.5   Symbols for objects used by the EPC method

It should be taken into account that (internal) 'events' have, in fact, already been described under the item 'result' of a message specification. This explains why 'events' are not present in the language and signs of the SqEME® approach. At the message specification 'order form' (see figure 7.5) the result could be mentioned as follows: 'To achieve that the client orders are received.' By marking the order form as an input to this process, the event – 'Client order received' is organized implicitly. The result of the 'Order confirmation' can be indicated as a result: 'To achieve that the client orders are confirmed', thus defining the next 'event' in the sequence.

7.2   Performance Indicators

Apart from the process flowcharts, the main part of the dashboard or scorecards of a process owner is 'covered' with solid management information about the processes concerned. Ensuring a healthy balance between their 'gut feeling' and the use of the management information system, the process owner keeps an eye on the operations as a whole and on their 'own' processes in particular.

An important aspect of process accountability is having performance indicators showing what to pay attention to in order to be able to monitor the business performance. Performance aspects can refer to quality, quantity, time and costs[51]. Think of aspects like processing time, waiting periods, dropouts, costs, client satisfaction and employee contentment. The description of a performance indicator is the starting point for defining measurements and the gathering of management information. Such a description should state which demands are made on its validity and reliability of the concerning management information.

---

[51] Tepper and Mulder (2002), *Kwaliteitsmanagement en resultaatgerichte bedrijfsvoering /RGB*

In addition, performance indicators are covered below, viewed in the light of the abstraction levels highlighted in the SqEME® method. Performance indicators can supply information on aspects of implementation (performing), about quality and coherence of the various business processes (designing), or about the course of the business process as a whole (governing).

The operations in our business process

Are our processes implemented properly? Do all resources contribute to the required result and are the agreements adopted in daily practice?

The process owner in the car company has measured the average period of time required per workshop assignment in order to prepare the job cards (planning board) and the work order file for use. This management information is about the fitness of people and resources for the specific processes and can, for instance, lead to the purchase of an automated planning- and workflow system. In this case, the business process in essence remains the same, on the condition that another automated mechanism is implemented, requiring less administrative load for the employees and thus also a smaller chance of errors.

The design of our business processes

Is the messaging, combined with the processes that are to be executed, suitable and robust enough to guarantee the quality of our products and services? What are the critical aspects of the business process, in the light of the mission of our organization?

In the car company the percentage of wrong diagnoses, becoming apparent during the repair, is being measured continuously. To guarantee the quality of the service, this performance indicator is labelled as one of the critical factors for success. When this part of the business process is not in control, and faults add up, it can be the reason to reconsider the way the organization handles the diagnosing and the management of the repair. It can also happen that the problem is of another 'dimension'. For example when it appears that the workshop chief wrongfully relies on the expertise of his employees and when he does not perform his regular check on the diagnostic results. It has to be asked why the agreed way of working is not being adopted in practice, after which adequate measures can be taken.

The aligning of the enterprise

What are we –as an enterprise- judged on by the customer and by other parties in the outside world? Is this fully taken into account in the overall constitution of the business? Is our Enterprise Architecture focussed sufficiently on the achievement of the external objectives?

As part of monitoring customer satisfaction, it should be established whether the newly-introduced collect and return service has had the expected positive effects. If this is the case, the decision will be made to not only introduce this service at Hyundai/Mitsubishi, but also for Fiat/Lancia. A measure like this has effects on the business process as a whole and should be carried out carefully.

The SqEME® method does not specify any conventions about the way of ordering or accessing performance indicators. Determining what are the performance indicators and linking them to the process architecture is expressly part of the method.

In terms of ordering performance indicators and making them accessible (management information), there is enough literature to be found. A popular framework for ordering financial and non-financial performance indicators is 'Balanced Scorecard' by Kaplan and Norton[52]. This model for a management information system derives objectives and performance indicators from the objective and the strategic policy of the organization. The results of the organization are judged from four perspectives: the financial perspective, the customer perspective, the perspective of the internal business processes and the learning and growth perspective. In this way, the attention of management should be balanced between external and internal indicators.

Another way of working to order and make accessible performance indicators has been developed by Kerklaan: namely the organization cockpit. Kerklaan describes the cockpit as a method for result-oriented management. It can be successfully applied in conjunction with the SqEME® method. The organization cockpit is based upon three principles: focus (vision, control-assignment and limited set of performance indicators), decomposition (strategy, search fields, performance criteria per search field) and 'ownership' (involvement of employees, relevant indicators and commitment)[53]. In his book, Kerklaan introduces the development and application of a measuring plan. With the measuring plan, a proper link can be made between processes on the one hand, and performance indicators and reporting about this on the other. The measuring plan consists of agreements about which indicators should be measured and how this should be done. The measuring plan is constructed by declaring per indicator what the criterion is, the standard, the measurement and recording system and the agreements about the reporting. It could also be indicated who is involved in generating the management information.

Execution of repairs			Result: perform repairs in accordance to agreements with customer	
Performance indicator	Standard	Measuring method/ measuring procedure	Way of analysing and reporting	Involved persons
1. Work supply (number of cars)	Not more than 2 cars are waiting for repair	Query in the registration system at: - check in time - start time engineers repair	[Branch] office report (weekly)	Team manager
2. Process time	A major overhaul requires 4 hours (average), a minor service 2 hours	Query in the registration system at: - start time engineers repair - time of delivery by mechanic	[Branch] office report (weekly)	Mechanic Team manager

Example 12.   Measuring plan for the conduct of repairs.

7.3   Tips & Tricks for the Correspondence window

Process flowcharts

Process flowcharts are clear and compact 'close-ups' of processes. It is necessary to follow some rules when creating them:

---

[52] Kaplan and Norton (1999), The balanced scorecard: translating strategy into action.
[53] Kerklaan (2006), *De cockpit van de organisatie*

- When working out a process, it is important to involve the stakeholders intensively. They can point out exactly which items are essential within the process and what agreements are necessary.
- Keep process flowcharts as simple as possible. One line of successive activities from top to bottom, documents to the left and right of this line. Use a five column structure; this provides a clear and uncomplicated view.
- The bounds of the process flowcharts (relationships with other processes) are based on the Key Result Area (interaction diagram).

| SUPPLIER (process) | INPUT | ACTIVITIES | OUTPUT | CUSTOMER (process) |

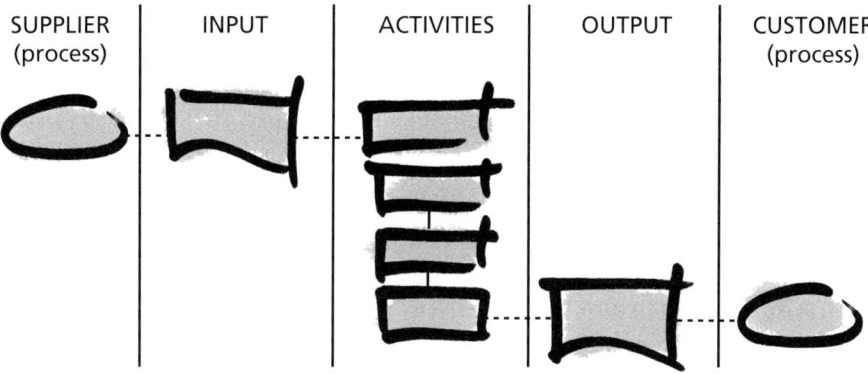

Figure 7.6   The five column structure of a process flowchart

- It is advisable not to include less than three or more than six activity boxes in one diagram. This limitation ensures that it is comprehensible.
- Only use four symbols: activity symbol, document symbol, connector symbol and linking arrows (see figure 7.2).
- Do not use decision-lozenges in the diagrams. Decisions are part of the activity and are –where necessary- described in the explanatory notes for an activity or in separate instructions. The final result of a decision is part of the message that is generated as an output of the corresponding activity.

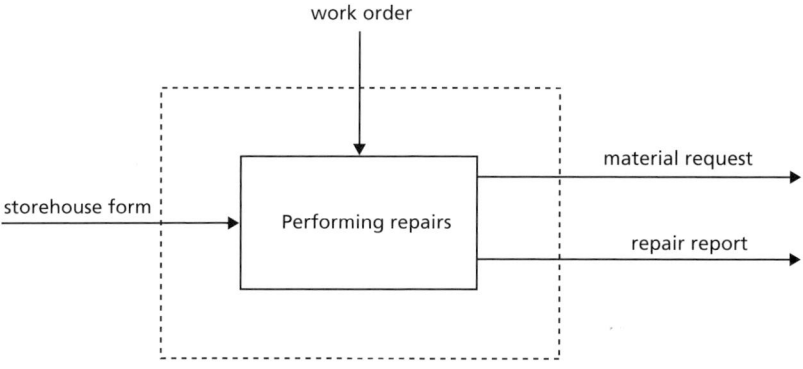

Example 13.   Bounds of the process flowchart 'executing repairs'.

- Do not mention actors in the explanatory notes with the activities. Who is involved in establishing the result concerned is mentioned in the message specification.
- A process description shows what happens, not how it happens. The latter is preferably left to the craftsmanship of the professional.
- How an activity should be performed, is (if necessary) described in separate protocols. Refer, where necessary, to the activity description in separate documents.
- When recording a process flowchart, start at the bottom right with the result of the process and work upwards. In this way, it is easy to concentrate on the 'main thread' of the process.
- Use as large a group of employees as possible in the development of process flowcharts in order to generate a better understanding of the working of the processes. Working out the process descriptions is a task especially meant for the company itself. Just having a process described with the process flowchart as the main goal is a missed opportunity. In particular, it is valuable to have a discussion about the processes that captures essential and critical issues that must be considered and agreed upon.
- To enhance the ease of understanding of the process flowchart it is sometimes unavoidable to refer to responsible people and applicable resources in the accompanying text. It is, however, not a major problem to do this. It just reduces the maintainability of the set of descriptions. Changing a resource or name of an actor means that this change will have to be made on both the process flowchart and on the message specification. The risk of unintentionally forgetting either or both of these is hard to eliminate.

Performance indicators
Some important clues for determining performance indicators are:
- In management reports, live by the principle of 'the dark cockpit of Boeing'. In an aeroplane, only those instruments requiring the pilot's attention are lit. As far as the rest are concerned, no news is good news. Though measurements take place, the results do not raise any alarm or they are not relevant at that time or in that specific situation.
- Objectives and standard values relating to the performance indicators are not a part of the language and signs of the SqEME® method. Because of the dynamics in this information, we categorize them with the operational data that the organization can agree upon in the message specifications.

7.4   Process Accountability in this window

The Correspondence window of the SqEME® method provides a view of the operation of the processes. What are the relevant performance indicators? What is the usual sequential execution of activities? And by means of which messages does a process relate to other processes both inside and outside the organization? To visualize and maintain the picture of the processes it is important that some aspects of process accountability are assigned and adjusted to the questions of this window mentioned above.

Dependent upon the complexity of the organization and the risks in the processes, in this window the process owner (formalized within the organization in whatever way) must be aware of the effective and efficient progress of the processes. It is an aspect of process accountability to carefully define and organize the 'points of measurement' to show the performance of the

enterprise. Within the framework of this window, aspects of process accountability are (amongst other things):
- knowing the process (processes) from beginning to end and mapping it (them);
- providing relevant management information about the process (processes) (by means of performance indictors, internal audits, external audits, complaints, ideas);
- making proposals to the line-management to improve the process;
- inspiring and initiating improvements to the process;
- if required, setting up an improvement work group;
- monitoring improvements.

This list is far from complete. In chapter 8 this list is used to further investigate the concept of process accountability. A key point in the SqEME® methodology is that the aspects mentioned above should not be assigned to just one person. For each aspect, it is worth discussing who the matter belongs to. This can be the internal controller, the quality manager, the IER officer, the operational manager, a member of the management team, etc. Also a separate (extra) role can be created to cover the aspects mentioned above, like a process coordinator, process owner or process manager.

8 Process Accountability

One of the most obvious differences between those enterprises that use process management as an approach to improve the quality of their organization and the ones that do not, is the presence of employees who are held accountable for (the quality of) these processes. For this reason, many organizations have appointed process owners or process managers. In practice, only a few organizations can get by easily with this new role in the organization. Seemingly, there are no standard solutions for handling process accountability. For example, in many organizations, one of the first challenges is having to make a decision on which tasks, powers and responsibilities a process owner should have. Lack of clarity about the distribution of authorities often blocks a successful implementation of process management.

This chapter looks in details at the way an organization could handle process accountability. Who in the organization is responsible for the quality of the processes? Which roles can be distinguished? How should the introduction of process accountability be handled? Which style matches that best?

8.1 From Processes as a Project to Process Management

Previous chapters have described how models can be developed and how a detailed understanding of the enterprise can be acquired from the different perspectives; the windows Constitution, Chemistry, Correspondence and Construction. These interaction diagrams, specifications and flowcharts are typically initiated as a result of a project-based approach. In a brief period of time, a lot of energy is put into achieving a tangible result. Simply having process flowcharts and interaction diagrams of Key Result Areas does not mean you have succeeded. After all, organizations are subject to changes like new technological opportunities (including those presented by ICT), changing legislation and rules, new insights into production or service, changes caused by movements in the market and new organization principles like Corporate Social Responsibility (CSR), that forces organizations to reconsider their processes.

Normally, describing and improving processes in an organization has a clear project structure. While working towards a clear goal, like certification of the operation on basis of the ISO 9001:2000, processes are being mapped and the necessary improvements are implemented. From the present way of working, an interaction diagram of the Key Result Area concerned is developed, the messages are worked out and deployed (in terms of the specific distribution of tasks and resources). Actually one makes a tour along the windows of the SqEME® approach to process management. For example, you can start from the Correspondence window, the initial condition of the processes, moving through the other windows, including several iterations, to arrive back at a renewed view through Correspondence window. This new state should match the objectives of the project. Therefore, this movement can be better described as a spiral movement rather than as a circular one. The project, under the leadership of the project manager, delivers enhancements to organization in terms of the specific execution of the processes and an increased process-awareness within the organization. After finalizing their project, the project manager hands over control to day-to-day management. If the spiral has been completed properly, the project manager will have to hand over the enhanced operation to a process owner, who may or may not be newly appointed. It is the task of this process owner to maintain and reinforce the spiral movement that has been initiated.

Process flowcharts and interaction diagrams of the Key Result Areas, and in particular the process awareness of employees, form a very valuable resource for an organization. In effect, they form the collective memory of shared pictures and agreements made about the way that work is carried out. Having these recorded process concepts offers lots of opportunities. They can, for example, be the starting point for the analysis, preparation and implementation of all kinds of changes. Finally, an important additional value can be found in the ability to use process management to work on the quality of the organization in a structured way: process management can be used to leverage organizational development.

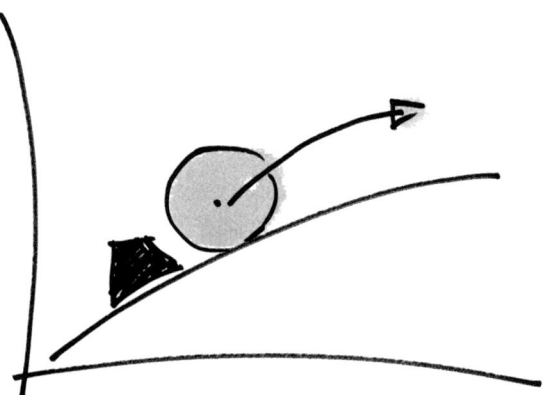

Figure 8.1   Meaning of process management in organizational development

A well-known metaphor about process enhancement is taken from an illustration in the ISO series, in which the ball represents the quality of the organization. An important notion in this is the question of what meaning process management can be given. Does process management have the significance of the wedge that keeps the ball in its place? Maintaining control of the organization, and the avoiding false steps and stumbles, as in quality assurance. Or does process management have quite the meaning of pushing the ball upwards the mountain? Feeling genuinely committed to the way of working? Small initiatives of individual employees on the work floor and larger improvement projects that make the organization grow? Apart from this 'in control' and 'continuous improvement' perspective, Bertrand Jouslin de Noray, currently the Secretary General of the European Organization for Quality (EOQ) has added two more perspectives. These are 'breakthrough', the actual breakthrough of the way in which the organization is perceived and thus how it is designed; and 'reaching the essence', the return to basics. What does this organization stand for? What drives us?

In the SqEME® method, process accountability signifies the feeling of responsibility for the quality of the organization. This vision of process accountability expresses itself most in the perspective of 'continuous improvement'. In a healthy organization, it is a role that people always take up implicitly. Feeling responsible for the quality of the organization is seated primarily in the value system and passion of people. Offering process management as a tool introduces the possibility of working on the organization and to assure it more explicitly and –if desired- also formally but in any case structurally. Process accountability means having a 'drive', feeling responsible for the way of working in the organization and wanting to continuously improve it.

8.2 Where People Work, Processes are Managed

Chapter 1 outlines the transition from the 'technological perspective' of the organization, originating the dominant type of organization that we named as the machine bureaucracy. The main principle of this type of organizing is the separation of thought and act. We have the working professionals and we have the thinking professionals. At this present time there is a tendency towards organizational forms based on the quality of the individual employees. In order to get the maximum out of these people – and also out of the cooperation between them- it is important that everyone thinks along the same lines about the approach to organizing processes. There should be no separation between thinking and working any more, with employees having a passion for their work, and taking the opportunity to talk over and think about the way in which processes can be optimally organized. This social system perspective makes organizations more flexible and better able to respond quickly to new situations. Process accountability translates this principle into practice. By explicitly assigning authority with regard to certain aspects of the quality of the organization, an infrastructure is created for the continuous improvement of the organization.

After all the social system perspective emphasises the importance of involving the right people in working on the organization. Employees who feel committed to the quality of the organization are explicitly asked to intervene on aspects of the quality of the organization. The essence of this is not having the best solution on paper; rather it is about mobilizing and facilitating the right people. In the words of the chairman of Microsoft, Bill Gates: 'How to bring resources to the problem'.

In every organization, including those where process accountability has not been explicitly assigned, work is being continuously undertaken on quality on a number of fronts – three of which will be mentioned later[54].

The individual people in the organization
Professional maturity of employees implies that they permanently have an eye for 'what can or has to be done better'. In a powerful organization, all employees can be expected to show initiative to implement improvements. Of course there are restrictions. As long as it is about individual ways of working it goes without saying that all people in the organization should be encouraged to contribute. On a yearly basis the amount of these kind of improvements is innumerable. They take place without formal assignment, budget and authority. In addition, there is no official

---

[54] Imai (1990), Kaizen – The Key to Japan's Competitive Success

notification of the result of the improvement result. It is the skills of management to enable these improvements 'to happen', to stimulate them and to reward their results.

Formal and informal groups

Yet when working methods and the design of the work are at issue, the initiation and implementation of improvements are more likely to be at a 'group level', in coalitions of like-minded people. To stimulate the development of these kind of improvements a company will have to purposefully create space and provide facilities. The number of improvements at this level will –for an average enterprise- run into hundreds. Implementing these kind of improvements can, dependent of the corporate culture, be given shape in a more or less formal structure of, for example, 'improvement working groups'. In this it is crucial that the group not only gets the authority to initiate things, but also –within limits- gets the responsibility for implementation.

Organization

Improvement projects initiated by line management who, at the same time, supervise the project organization concerned, are much less numerous than the types of improvements outlined in the two levels mentioned above. However, only ten to twenty of these kinds of projects within an organization can generate substantial dynamics! There are radical consequences for the design of the organization, the deployment, and/or reconsideration of the Enterprise Architecture, and the messages communicated within the organization. These kinds of projects affect the policy of the organization and, in many cases, significant costs are involved. Because of these reasons, only management can be accountable for the accomplishment of such improvement projects.

The assignment of project responsible is a measure that manifests itself at group level, but in particular at the organization level, as just described. As a consequence, the manner in which management deal with process enhancement should be structured and formalized for maximum benefit. In defining the 'focus and scope' of the process owners, it is important to manage the expectations of the 'workers in the organization' properly. If both the organization as a whole, and the process owner in particular, are insufficiently aware of the fact that the majority of the improvements are achieved on an informal level of the organization, the danger exists that the desire and energy to improve will flow out of the organization as a result of this perception 'We have a process owner, so everything will turn out all right!'

Consequently, an appointed process owner would be wise to – in addition to their role of providing direction for improvement initiatives at the management level- concentrate on stimulating the self-learning abilities of the organization as a whole. The capacity of an organization to distinguish itself from the others will often increasingly manifest itself in the way that it is able to provide people with the space and opportunity to contribute to the way of organizing. Is the organization able to address its social and intellectual power and to develop it? The way in which an organization chooses to handle process accountability will, in practice, be closely related to the phase of development that it is in. Because of this, process accountability will be viewed in a different way in every organization. It is important, therefore, that the employees within an organization mutually discuss what is the best approach to take.

8.3 There are Various Styles of Process Management

Feeling part of the way everything passes off in an organization, and how this might be improved, is an attitude of every professionally mature employee. Therefore, the basis of process management is to be found primarily in the passion of people. Because people differ, this passion does not always find expression in the same way, people have different value systems[55]. Elaborating on the pragmatic 'colour thinking' of De Caluwé and Vermaak[56] we illustrate process accountability in colour in the following overview:

- The yellow process owner focuses on bringing together interests. By forming coalitions they purposefully work towards a win-win situation, with the exact result not known in advance.
- The blue process owner works as a project manager to achieve a previously carefully specified process improvement. They are an expert on the matter and work towards a demonstrably better and assured process quality.
- The red process owner concentrates on the operational workers in the process. Through the application of HRM instruments (assessing and rewarding), employees are encouraged to work towards a previously devised process improvement.
- The green process owner devotes themselves to providing complete and reliable process information to management and operational staff. They are convinced that constructive feedback is the ultimate means of achieving the continuous improvement of processes. In effect, learning by doing.
- The white process owner puts in effort as a pure facilitator of the success of the workers in the process. They are constantly busy creating space and energy for experiments, resulting in surprising improvements.

It should be noted that any particular value system is not necessarily superior to another. It is better to investigate which style is the most appropriate at a particular time and in a specific part of the company. Anyhow, experience has shown that companies tend to select the 'green process owner' when introducing process management. This is based upon the idea that providing good management information to professionals will ensure that process management gains a proper place in the concept of control of the organization as a result of demonstrating identifiable successes.

8.4 It is a Choice to Formalize Process Accountability

The way the management of the organization handle process accountability depends on the desired dynamics and energy in improving processes. The *INK-managementmodel* links the conscious control and governing of process quality (criterion nr. 5) to the phases of development –the degrees of complexity or maturity- of an organization. The *INK-managementmodel* distinguishes a 'phase III' in which an organization is characterized by a system orientation, it is aware of the entire spectrum of business processes and their relation. A 'phase III' organization has formally addressed the control of processes by assigning process owners. Also ISO 9001:2000 seeks to formalize process accountability.

---

[55] www.spiraldynamics.net
[56] Léon de Caluwé en Hans Vermaak, Leren veranderen, Kluwer, 2002

When an organization decides to explicitly assign process owners, this indicates that the leaders are serious about what they are planning to achieve. The organization not only wants to have the quality of products under control, but they explicitly focus attention and create space to invest more in the quality of their processes.

	Phase I Activity oriented	Phase II Process oriented	Phase III System oriented	Phase IV Value Chain oriented	Phase V Excel and transform
5a Identifying and designing	There is an organization diagram, showing all departments and positions	Primary processes and the steps to be distinguished are described	All processes and their mutual relationships are systematically described	The links between the internal processes and those of the clients and partners are mapped	mumsel*
5b Implementing and controlling	Management determines the way of working and supervises this	The quality of the primary processes is a accountability that goes beyond departments	Employees with result accountability delegate authority for the implementation and control of processes to process owners	Cooperation in the value chain is organized with the process owners of clients and partners	mumsel*
5c Analyzing and improving	Complaints and deviations are the reasons to improve working methods	Management information leads to planned and budgeted improvement projects	Through the use of management information, process owners stimulate the process of continuous improvement at all levels	Innovation and improvement of cooperation is structurally worked on with clients and partners	mumsel*

* A mumsel is something many people talk about but no one has ever seen

Figure 8.2   Phases of development in process management (based on the INK-managementmodel).

It will have a very practical advantage for many organizations in creating an infrastructure for the purpose of governing and improving processes. This is particularly relevant for more complex organizations, in which the processes do not have a one-to-one relationship with the organizational sections or departments. There can be specific processes that are executed in one or more department that play an important role in the execution of one common process.

When agreements have to be made in these complex organizations about the development and deployment of processes, it implies discussions between many line managers and consequently the need for formal approval by a higher authority. Through the naming and assigning of various aspects of process accountability, particularly to others then the line managers, the workload on the existing hierarchical structures can be relieved. The main part of the process alignment between the different departments can then be controlled by the process owners, without the need to involve the senior management.

In the business case of the car company, there are four different brands of cars. All these brands have their own spare parts supply. The car company is organized in such a way that every brand has its own senior management that has overall accountability for managing the related part of the warehouse. Process accountability is named and assigned in such a way that one of the four senior managers is explicitly assigned the role of mutually aligning, tuning and improving the processes. Subsequently, it is the responsibility of this person to authorise which changes will be implemented under his control!

8.5 Accountability for Processes is Arranged Differently Than for Results

An important development in process thinking is distinguishing between process accountability and result accountability. It is also important to recognize that process accountability is not merely an aspect of result accountability! Most importantly, it offers a completely different dimension through which to look at the organization. Result accountability refers to the obligation to give an account of the result of the effort. Process accountability refers to an authority and to a right to intervene with respect to a certain aspect of the quality of organizing processes[57].

The organizational concept of franchising is a fine example with which to explain the phenomena of process accountability and result accountability. The franchisee, for example the branch manager of a supermarket, is fully result responsible and –just like any other entrepreneur- runs the risk of going bankrupt. The franchiser is also result responsible and has a number of shared tasks under his management (on behalf of all of the affiliated supermarkets), like purchase and marketing and has overall accountability for these. This distribution of authorities is carefully recorded with respect to both parties. So, the franchisee has delegated the authority for designing the organization of their company to the franchiser. Think of how the personnel are trained, how stock is controlled, or how marketing is organized. This is an aspect of process accountability that is a part of the franchise contract. In this way the entrepreneur can focus entirely on their primary task; serving their customer.

All too often the assignment of process accountability is linked to 'shifting' the structure of the organization from e.g. a product or market orientation towards an orientation on processes[58]. In itself, there is no objection to organizing process accountability as a separate role, or even as a department if this is justified by the complexity of the organization. However, in the case of such a shift of the organization structure, the distinction between result accountability and process accountability is not considered. The shift boils down to the assignment of result accountability, no longer in terms of vertical hierarchical departments, often a bundling of expertise, but in terms of the horizontal organization. Line managers are now grouped according to the lines of the processes. The resulting change of the structure is actually represented by a renewed, shifted, organization chart. Basically it involves a lot of juggling with positions and roles. The result is a process organization (or a matrix organization) in which the workflow is controlled via the horizontally assigned result responsibilities. Vertical responsibilities in this case are (partially) about ensuring that (properly trained) employees are made available. Whether the 'vertical' or the 'horizontal' manager has the employees and the resources at their disposal is a matter that is still in dispute. In brief: who has the budget? In practice, lots of organizations wrestle with this issue.

---

[57] Ahaus (2005), Dialoog over bevoegdheid en verantwoordelijkheid
[58] INK (2004), Organisatieontwikkeling van fase II naar fase III

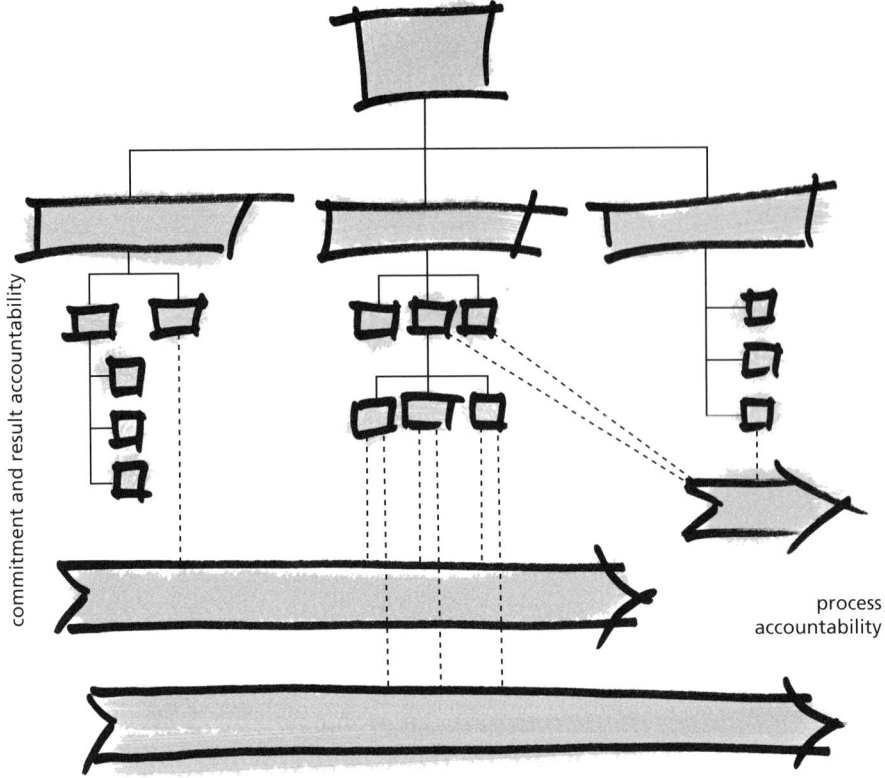

Figure 8.3　Relationship between process accountability and result accountability

Process owners are assigned, but what do they exactly do? Do we now have two people to report to? Organizations have difficulties with this tilting perspective. Many people will be frustrated rather than helped by this solution. Matrix structures, that start from this approach, are also complex solutions that do not work.

In the approach mentioned above, tilting is handled as a change of structure. The crux of the matter is that this tilting perspective does not distinguish between result accountability and process accountability. The SqEME® approach does not encourage a change of the organization structure, but rather it asks for another way of looking at the organization. Where we are used to control the primary processes, to supervise them and make them predictable by means of the hierarchy (regardless of whether it was organized vertically or horizontally), we now set up a(n) (infra)structure in which we can discuss the quality of the organization: who cooperates with whom? In this, process accountability is concerned with the improvement of processes in the organization. Process owners are actors in these improvement processes, a role they have in addition to the position they already occupy within the organization. This introduces an extra degree of complexity in organizing! The tilting has a particularly large impact on the way that people cooperate with each other and how they deal with the organization (5). In this sense, process accountability is at least as much about 'feeling responsible' as it is about the technical discussion of who should really be held responsible on the basis of their authority. This vision of process accountability can be traced back to the basics of 'inclusive thinking'. It calls for articulate employees who devote themselves pro-actively to the quality of the work and cooperation; the horizontal organization.

A shift of the mindset

Process accountability also exists in value chains and in networks. At her website, Anja van der Aa (of the virtual platform chains and networks) writes about this: 'Value chains are often presented as organizations that have shifted to a process orientation, but the essence is a shift of the mindset. A shift from a dominantly hierarchical structure to a more horizontally organized society. Behind cooperation concepts like value chains, supply chains, networks, alliances, clusters, etc, hides a system change that slowly develops. The enormous turnaround that is finally made consists of:

- from assigning accountabilities to proactively taking responsibility and initiative;
- from talking in policy processes (words) to an orientation focused on primary processes (acting);
- from working from policy objectives to a problem and question centred focus and attitude;
- from planning/structuring to governing and organizing dynamic teamwork;
- from centralizing institutions/organizations to centralizing people (professionals and clients) with the potential to develop;
- from laying down rules/procedures to facilitating new working procedures with ICT (learning, sharing knowledge and exchanging information);
- from developing and discussing a lot to cooperating and bundling peoples own added value.

Where one actually talks of value chains and networks, whilst still thinking in fixed positions, it goes wrong. After all, anyone who does not want to adapt will persevere with their old behaviour. Those who succeed in making the mental shift will be successful in cooperating. For the ones who want to but are not able, there is simple advice: stop doing the things that do not work today. This creates space to think another way!

It will be clear that the implementation of a governance structure for organizational quality is not a project that can be finalized in a spare hour. It is a 'power shift'[60]. In the traditional forms of organization both responsibilities are often assigned to the same person, the line manager. The senior managers in an organization will take no risks when assigning specific authority with respect to the design of the process. It requires a firm basis of trust and commitment before they will give others (usually the more qualified experts) more space to optimally organize the processes they manage everyday, within precisely defined frameworks.

8.6 The Scope of a Process owner

The conclusion of the preceding section is that the explicit assignment of process accountability is an extra degree of complexity for the organization. This accountability is an upshot of the fact that authority in relation to working on the quality of the organization is assigned from line managers to other specifically involved individuals.

---

[60] Toffler (1990), Powershift, chapter 18

The things that a person with specific process responsibilities can really be called to account for depend upon the authority they have been given or have acquired from the result responsible person. The role that a process owner can claim has a variety of possibilities. Through chapters 4 to 7 we have partially defined this gamut already. The aspects of process accountability mentioned were:

With respect to the Constitution window:
• making agreements about the principles of the organization (mission/vision/ strategy/ policy) and translating them intoto Key Result Areas and processes;
• making critical results clearly visible within the Key Result Areas (the croquet wickets);
• creating an overview;
• striving to evolve the mental processes in the organization from 'departmental thinking' to 'process, system and value chain thinking.'

With respect to the Chemistry window:
• making agreements on the quality of the information supply;
• making agreements about demonstrable conformity to preconditions such as the standard series ISO 9001, ISO 14001, ISO 18001, HACCP, SCC, SOX, etc.;
• ensuring comprehension, coherence and interdependency between the various processes.

With respect to the Construction window:
• assigning (operational) tasks, responsibilities and authorities;
• separating the functions;
• adjusting the roles to the existing job descriptions;
• having performance interviews with employees;
• assigning the budget;
• taking care of the training and education of employees;
• taking care of the introduction of ICT, forms, etc.;
• making tacit of knowledge available in knowledge systems (where necessary);
• taking necessary measures and developing the resources that are necessary for the execution and control of work.

With respect to the Correspondence window:
• understanding the processes from the start to the end and mapping them;
• providing relevant and reliable management information about the process or processes, through the use of performance indicators, internal audits, external audits, complaints, ideas etc.;
• making suggestions to line management about how processes might be improved;
• inspiring and initiating improvements in the process;
• establishing an improvement working group, if desired;
• following and monitoring the implementation of improvements.

For each of these aspects it is worth discussing where in the organization they should be assigned and who should claim the leadership (or already has it in practice). In an organization in which the role of process owner is not yet explicitly assigned to someone, line management remains fully authorized to intervene in the process design of the department in question. The result accountable manager is also process owner. In many organizations, aspects are assigned to staff members anyway. Tasks can, for instance, be assigned to the quality manager, the controller, or in some organizations to the ICT department. In many organizations a number of the tasks mentioned are assigned to positions established specifically for this purpose, like the process owner or the process manager.

The redistribution of these tasks and authorities can be initiated by the executive or by higher management. For processes that take place in identical ways in different departments, like a decentralized purchase authority, then 'top management' can, of course, appoint a process owner as an interlocutor for several department managers. This can also apply to processes - designated by the organization - that exceed the bounds of the departments.

In case of a franchise organization, the authorities of both the franchiser and the franchisee have been carefully defined and documented in the franchise contract. A similar mechanism (a sort of franchise contract) is a critical success factor for the introduction of process management. The senior management in the organization would be wise to unambiguously agree upon and record the expectations with respect to the process owners, including the process responsibilities that are delegated to them. This warning also works the other way! Do not say 'yes' to the question of whether you would like to have the title of process manager, owner, coordinator or any other distinguished title, if the expectations and the authority that come with this role are not perfectly clear. Furthermore, it is wise to handle the appointment of process owners on an individual basis and to reach a compromise between the 'ideal' and the 'practicable' in certain cases. When introducing process management, practice has taught us that there are several areas available for a process owner to exercise their influence.

Yet, the start point is crucial. To enable a process owner to work on the quality of the organization successfully, then as a minimum the following three authorities will have to be allocated to the individual concerned:
- Access to management information. The process owner must have (physical) access to all information that is relevant to the analysis of the process concerned. This means that the process owner must be able to move 'freely' throughout the organization units where this process is executed.
- Formulating objectives. The process owner must be able to confirm which key performance indicators and accompanying goals should, in their opinion, be applicable to the process. They should, for instance, be able to put this on the agenda for the management meeting of the organization and, in this way, draw the attention to relevant improvement issues in the business process.
- Initiating working groups. The process owner must have the mandate to gather together the concerning employees and managers for at least one day in order to discuss an improvement proposition that is clearly defined and has been prepared by the process owner.

On the basis of the above, the conditions are created whereby the process owners can create a distinct profile for themselves over time in their new role on the basis of proven success. Usually, when a process manager proves to be successful they typically gain trust and consequently acquire additional authority, in particular leadership. It should be noted that 'authority' is the key concept rather than 'responsibility', because the real transfer of authority determines whether the process owner is really accountable (for the quality of the process) or if they just 'feel responsible'.

8.7   Process roles With a Different Scope

According to the SqEME® method, process management is something that concerns all the people within an organization. The SqEME® approach starts from the concept that, just as in leadership, this role can be picked up by anyone in the organization. Process management is not necessarily linked to the vertical hierarchical structure of the organization. Primarily, it is an aspect of the corporate culture and must be inherited in the drive of the people. Process accountability will appear in different shapes for each organization. It is up to the organization to come to agreements about the way in which process accountability is shaped. Do we want to separate process accountability from result accountability and –if so- within which scope do we expect the process owner to develop initiatives? Here, the term 'scope' means the specific selection of tasks and authorities that are delegated by line management at the point at which the process role in question is created. The gamut of aspects of process accountability described in the previous section offers a helping hand in carrying out this conversation effectively and choosing the required scope (i.e. making a selection). Even though the list of aspects might be extensive, it still supplies an incomplete overview. When introducing the role of process accountability within their own ranks, organizations are free to add extra aspects to the list, or to shorten it or redefine it. To bring the role of process accountability to life and to ease the way it is embedded within the organization, the list of aspects from the previous section can be fleshed out with a number of examples of process roles. These roles are not obligatory, but they can help to stimulate process accountability in the organization. In this case, one also has to check whether the list is satisfactory for each separate role. Depending on the desired scope, aspects might have to be redefined, or even assigned elsewhere!

Possible process roles and their scope are:
The process coach (a senior manager):
- making agreements about the principles of the organization (mission/vision/strategy/policy) and translating them into the Key Result Areas and processes;
- striving to enable the thinking process in the organization to grow from 'department thinking' to 'process, system and value chain thinking';
- increasing the understanding of the need for coherence and dependence between the various processes;
- maintaining the overview with regard to the process organization.

The process owner (can be anyone in the organization, but it is usually a line manager):
- knowledge of the process(es) from the start to the end and their mapping;
- making the critical results within the process (the croquet wickets) clearly visible;
- inspiring and initiating improvements in the process;
- setting up of improvement working groups (if desired);
- following and monitoring the implementation of improvements.

The process architect (quality manager, controller or process advisor):
- mapping and describing the processes;
- making agreements on the quality of the information supply;
- making agreements on the demonstrable compliance to preconditions such as the standard series ISO 9001, ISO 14001, ISO 18001, HACCP, SCC, SOX, etc.;
- making arrangements and ensuring that the necessary resources are available to undertake the work;
- developing suggestions for improvements in the process.

The process expert (everyone in the organization):
- understanding and mapping the process(es) from the start to the end;
- documenting the craftsmanship in knowledge systems (where necessary);
- developing suggestions for improvements in the process.

The process coordinator (often the controller or their employee(s)):
- ensuring the availability of relevant and reliable management information about the process(es) by means of performance indicators, internal audits, external audits, complaints, ideas etc.;
- developing suggestions for improvements in the process.

The process manager (the line manager):
- distributing the (operational) tasks, responsibilities and authorities;
- carrying out job performance interviews with employees;
- assigning the budgets;
- addressing the training and education requirements of employees;
- co-ordinating the introduction of ICT, forms, etc.

8.8   The Focus of a Process owner

The area in which a supervisor of a department or team may exercise their powers is clearly marked out, often even by walls and doors: 'This is the area that I manage, these are my people and my machines'. If we look at one of the roles described above for the process owner, we can see that this is literally much more abstract. In order to describe their area of attention, their 'focus', one always has to fall back on the abstract models based upon concrete reality. In many cases organizations make the boundaries of the 'playground' of the process owner clear by linking their authority to one or more of the process flowcharts that are conceived in the Correspondence window. If there is a need to refine the focus, the process accountability can be agreed on the basis of each message specification. Laying down the process accountability per Key Result Area in turn leads to a less-specific distribution. The larger the playground, the easier it will be to manage the coherence. A smaller playground can lead to significant interference in relation to the content, with the risk that the process will not be undertaken in an optimum manner. For this reason, in large organizations the control concept regarding the quality of the organization is built up from several process roles. For example, process coordinators can be assigned for each message specification and they are made responsible for gathering the management information on the relevant part of the business process. These process coordinators report to, and are supervised by, process owners who have been given the task of mapping the quality of the organization against each Key Result Area, and to intervene if necessary, within strict guidelines.

The roles described above are significant. They are undertaken by a relatively senior employee, for instance by a line manager who is committed to a certain process, or by a quality manager who feels involved with a number of the aspects mentioned from their own perspective. It also happens that organizations create new positions or departments to embed process management successfully. Often these are process advisors who support line managers in the continuous improvement of the business, having a large number of the aspects described above assigned to them. These process advisors form the link not only between the process owners, but also often with the quality manager or the controller on the one side and other persons involved, such as ICT employees and personnel managers, on the other. It also happens that specific groups or teams are established to discuss the impact upon the organization, for instance the so-called 'quality circles' or 'user groups'. In general, the rule applies that the assignment of functionaries is only required if justified by the complexity of the business case. Otherwise we will start by involving the right people. In other words, we create the infrastructure right through the organization!

8.9   Special Attention for the 'Process Auditor'

The person auditing the processes in the organization has a special bond with process accountability. Depending on the assignment of management, the process auditor is expected to fulfil the role of the expert, or they are the one holding up an objective mirror in front of the process owners and the operational workers.

In the first case, a process audit can also be done by external professional auditors who are experts themselves, or by auditors guided by experts on the matter. The essential fact is that the external auditor passes judgement about the organization. They investigate whether the organization meets the necessary requirements to operate within the market.

In the second case, where the process auditor holds up the mirror for the organization, the role of auditor can be perfectly well performed by one of their own employees, an internal auditor. In internal audits like this, one investigates the robustness of processes and whether their execution is in conformity with agreed procedures. Through an investigation like this, one can tell what processes in the organization are executed in conformity to how they are planned and where the weaknesses, the potential points of improvement, are located. In this sense, process auditing is a planned review of the (established) routines in the business process at a given point in time. Processes are closely monitored without an immediate cause being present.

The approach is to critically investigate the system of working. Process auditing is a safety net for the process owner, in much the same way as having performance interviews forms a safety net for an operational manager. Ideally, a manager should continuously and constructively supply their employees with feedback. However, the hectic daily schedule may leave little time to deal with this. For this reason it is wise to have a planned meeting for management, at least annually, where they gather around the table and evaluate the performance.

Also a process owner should continuously observe things in a critical fashion and consider whether it is wise to implement improvements in the system of cooperating.

Daily practice leaves little room for this, so a system of internal auditing can at least ensure this one annual review per process. In this way it can form an important source of management information.

The execution of internal audits, therefore, is an important issue in ISO 9001:2000. To management, in their roles both as formal process accountable and as client of the process audits, it yields interesting information about how the organization is performing. If an organization decides to organize internal process audits and trains internal auditors for that purpose, the knife cuts both ways. Because the internal auditors are asked explicitly to critically and constructively examine the how processes are undertaken for themselves and for the organization as a whole, they will contribute to a greater awareness of the processes in the organization and their coherence. In many organizations, putting in place an internal auditing instrument is a very practical point of crystallization for process management. The structure for commissioning assignments to carry out internal process audits, their execution and the subsequent reporting, if carefully designed and aimed at 'learning by doing', then forms a practical basis for process driven operation.

9 A Tool for a Process Driven Approach

This chapter is about the way in which we can apply the SqEME® approach to process management to handle organizational and managerial issues. After all, the SqEME® approach to processes is not an objective itself, but is meant to be used as a tool. In chapters 4 through to 7, the method has been explained per window as a set of instruments; the hammer and all the other tools of the carpenter. This chapter successively covers nine examples of issues for the process-centred approach, for which SqEME® as a toolkit, can be applied successfully. In each case we will describe the steps for handling the question and what this means for the contribution of each window. For each step we illustrate how one can handle the descriptions and the corresponding language and signs. When organizations are looked at through process-spectacles they manifest themselves differently, so some of the questions are accompanied by a reflection on further opportunities that the centralizing of processes could bring with it.

9.1 The Organization Wants to be Certified

The question of certification, the need to assure quality and, if desired, to have it rewarded with a certificate is an issue for many organizations. The key point is that the organization demonstrably complies with requirements. The SqEME® approach calls these requirements the preconditions to be allowed to operate in the market, the 'license to operate'. Think of ISO 9001, the Working Conditions Act, which is packed with requirements on the subject of environmental control, financial management and so on. In order to realize this 'transparency', it is important to know what requirements are addressed (1), to decide which processes they apply to (2), to find out whether the measures have been taken to comply to these requirements (3) and to determine whether these measures are sufficiently assured and demonstrable (4). In figure 9.1 these steps have been illustrated as a walk along the windows.

1. Which requirements are we talking about?
In practice, there is more than one set of requirements. You may, for example, wish to comply with requirements on the subject of quality care, safety, health and environment. Gathering and working through these standards and guidelines yields a collection of preconditions for the business process, such as 'Our measurement devices are calibrated', with reference to the related source document.

2. To which verb, which process, does each requirement apply?
In the list of preconditions, one can consequently make an inventory of those processes that enable the requirement to be met. For example, the precondition on the measurement equipment plays a role in all processes that require the use of measuring devices and in which the control and the availability of the devices is taken care of. For the purpose of compiling this inventory, it is clear that having a Enterprise Architecture with the underlying Key Result Area descriptions is of great help in quickly determining the impact of the requirement on the business process.

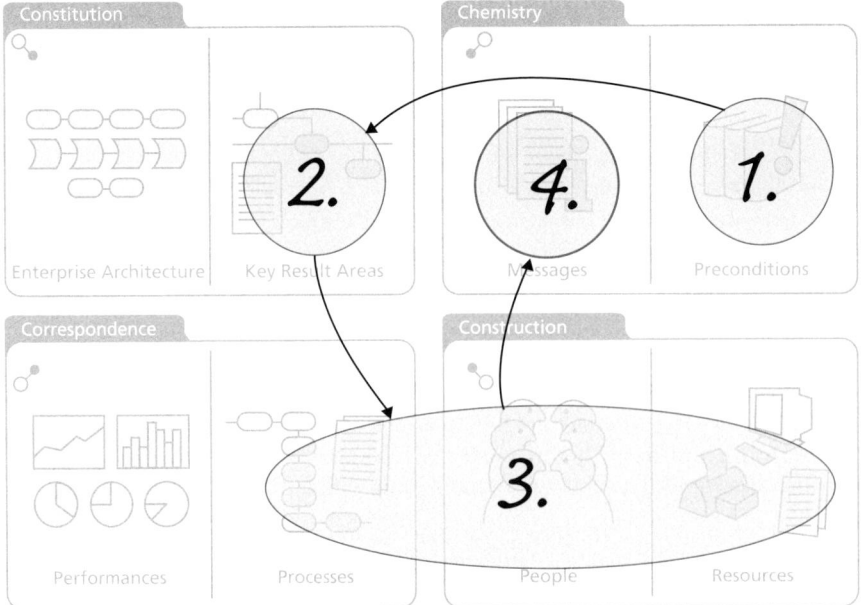

Figure 9.1   The issue of certification

3. Do we comply with all requirements?

Looking at the existing process flowcharts for each process on the list, talking to the people responsible for carrying these out and checking the present way of working, provides a view on the degree of compliance with the requirements. This exercise can also be completed with audits or other techniques of verification. Based on this inventory, the process flowcharts can be adjusted to the desired situation, people can be instructed or the necessary adaptations made to the resources, and the system of regulations can be carried through.

4. Are the measures assured and demonstrable?

A judgement needs to be made on whether the present registrations objectively verify if the correct working procedures are being adopted for the specific processes so that compliance is achieved with the requirements. In this example, the main issues are that the calibration reports of the measurement means are available, it is possible to check which particular device has been used for a performed measurement, etc. By studying the message specifications, it can be verified whether agreements have been concluded on these registrations. If necessary, dependent upon the outcome, selected administrative measures can be taken that are important for verifiability and assurance purposes. A certification program, like that just described, can be finalized by establishing a matrix that indicates how, for every precondition, the organization demonstrably complies to the requirements by means of specific messages (refer to example 7 in section 5.2).

9.2   The Organization Wants to Realize an Improvement

Problems or ambitions with respect to the performance of the internal organization can always be translated into processes. In a process driven organization, this can even be the start point. The questions and the corresponding passage along the windows have the following pattern: what is the problem or the ambition (1), in which processes are we going to intervene (2), who can we involve in this (3), what specific investments are necessary (4) and how can we check whether we are successful (5).

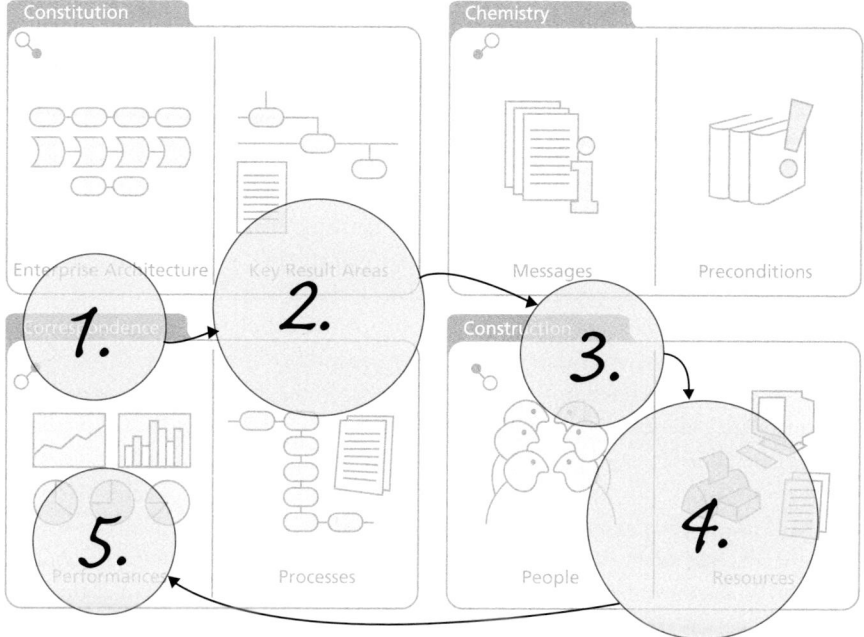

Figure 9.2   Realising an improvement

1. What is the problem or the ambition?
A vague notion expressed in terms like 'couldn't this be done cheaper?' or the fact that management information shows that delivery periods are being exceeded across the structure, can be the reason to start an improvement project. Depending upon how well defined the reason is, a direction for the improvement can be indicated in the Enterprise Architecture, or the specific objective can be formulated in the management information system. In the latter case the improvement course can be handled on a strict project base. In the first case an approach of 'learning renewal' is better suited.

2. In which processes are we going to intervene?
Apart from the definition of the cause, there is a requirement to identify where an intervention is most 'profitable'. For this purpose one can first explore the question through the use of an Ishikawa diagram or a mind map. The Enterprise Architecture, the Key Result Areas and the process flowcharts form an important means of interpreting the question, depending on how well defined the question is. In case one wants to shorten the 'process times' they can be documented in the process flowcharts. Awkward dependencies and conflicting interests can be put in the Enterprise Architecture or in the Key Result Area descriptions, for example 'How can we – taking into account the uncertainties of the sales process - still plan production as effectively as possible and reduce equipment change periods?'.

3. Who to involve?
Guided by an illustration of the question and its relationship with the processes, it is clear which expertise has to be mobilized. This is a strategic choice in terms of the extent to which operational workers and supervisors should be involved in the improvement process. Looking at the processes it should be clear who in the organization will be impacted. By, for instance, rewriting the process flowcharts, the desired situation can be described. If that desired situation has consequences for more processes, their coherence and the distribution of tasks, then it means that job descriptions and message specifications have also to be rewritten in order to correspond with the desired situation.

4. Where to invest in?
Tackling the question in conjunction with experts and deciding what would be the correct working method is a good start and, in fact, means that half the job is done. The other half starts off with the question of what is necessary to implement the new working method. Are any adjustments in the work instructions desired, how do we brief the employees, does the training need to be revised or organized, what does the new way of working mean for ICT? Using the matrix relationships between resources and processes or messages, the impact of the new working method can be analysed. The 'ticked' process flowcharts and message specifications can be used to focus precisely on alterations to existing resources, or on the need to organize specific training.

5. Is the success of the improvement verifiable and assured?
The project can be finalized when the implementation of the new working methods has resulted in the achievement of the formulated objectives. If they have not been agreed upon at the start of the improvement project, it should at least have become clear during the project what the resultant benefits should be. It is worthwhile explicitly highlighting this in the management information system in order to collect the benefits that arise out of the completion of a job like this, and to consequently communicate these to all people involved.
Upon completion of the job, the responsibility for the new working method is handed over from the project organization to the appropriate process owner(s) in the existing organization.

9.3 The Organization Wants More Attention for Continuous Improvement

Thinking in processes helps an organization when they want to invest in their 'learning abilities' and when they want to focus on the requirement to continuously improve in the work that is being done. Thinking in processes offers the employees the possibility to distinguish between working *in* and working *on* the organization. One thinks of processes when considering how the work is organized and whether there are opportunities to improve the organization of the work. It is important that every employee in the organization starts from the same suppositions, and that their views match. It is particularly in this field that the SqEME® approach can contribute considerably to gaining an overview and insight into the ins and outs of the organization,. To stimulate continuous improvement in an organization it is necessary to: have a thorough view of the essence of the organization, the verbs required to accomplish the mission and to know which of these are critical and why (1), to discuss with each other who in the organization claims responsibility for which processes (2), who devotes himself to this and what means are available (3) and how we monitor the processes and continue to improve (4).

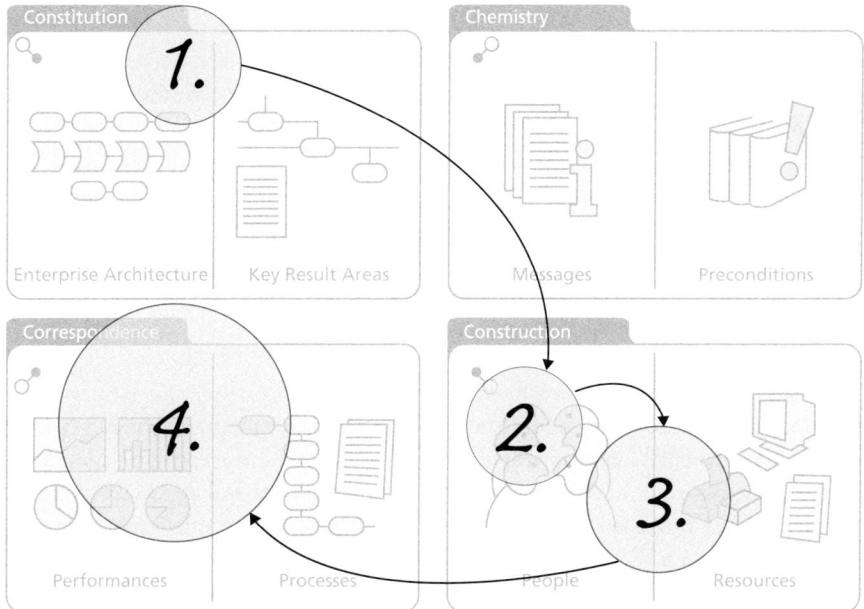

Figure 9.3   Attention for continuous improvement

1. Which processes reflect the essence of the work?

Continuous improvement depends on the initiative of the individual employee or the group. Because it is not based on a clear director's function, it is of importance to provide guidance and to 'frame' these initiatives. Developing the Enterprise Architecture is a useful tool for this purpose. Naming the most important verbs of the organization and , for example, writing them on sticky notes and putting them on a 'storyboard' visible for everyone, can enable all employees to work on a shared picture of the architecture of the enterprise. Subsequently, this architecture can be developed further in separate working groups and in accordance with the establishment of Key Result Area descriptions. These working groups can be allocated the authority to name and communicate the interfaces with other working groups and to address the critical success factors within their 'own' Key Result Area. In this way those involved, usually the management team and middle management, develop a true shared description of the process architecture of the organization over a period of just a few weeks. This 'big picture' can then serve as a platform, a process map, for further developments and investments, as well as for the more formal distribution of the aspects of process accountability.

2. Who claims which aspect of process accountability?

If the Enterprise Architecture and the Key Result Area interaction diagrams have a certain robustness (are basically stable), then one can decide who in the organization accepts the accountability for assuming or coordinating the improvement initiatives for each distinct process. In order to achieve this, one can think of several ways of working. A very lively one is a so-called 'claim and grant session'. Take a large meeting room and pin up A2-sheets with the Key Result Area descriptions and let everyone stick notes on the building blocks where they want some involvement. Then discuss as a group what image this creates. Why do some Key Result Areas remain empty and why do initiatives manifest themselves in other Key Result Areas? What does this tell us about the work and about the way that process owners obviously look at it? After the discussion one can finally 'divide the loot' and identify the process roles as explained in section 8.7. During this session, it is important to explicitly agree the framework within which one is expected to fulfil these process roles.

3. Which resources have to be provisioned?

The assigned process owners can be asked to produce a brief plan to explain how they want to fulfil their role within the previously determined framework and what resources they think they need. This can refer to the availability and time required of employees, or to specific resources they wish to introduce in order to improve the process.

4. How to perpetuate continuous improvement?

By asking the process owners how they want to account for their investments, the basis is created for further development of the management information system or, for example, a Business Balanced Scorecard[61]. As well as addressing the requirements of accountability, disclosing this management information can also have a stimulating effect. It can start off an improvement competition, the desire to excel in realizing process improvements. By also documenting the realized improvements, a system of internal auditing can contribute to the durable character of the achieved improvements. The internal auditing of processes itself can also generate extra 'improvement energy'.

9.4 The Organization Wants to Reorganize

For various reasons, one can decide to adjust the 'construction of the organization'. Think of a merger or acquisition, an enormous growth in sales, or political intervention in a governmental organization. To implement this reorganization it has to be clear exactly what change is required (1), for which processes it has consequences (2), to what extent it influences the distribution of tasks and the interaction between processes (3), which resources should be developed or readjusted to help successfully achieve the reorganization (4), what that specifically implies for the operation (5) and how we can control the transition from 'old' to 'new' (6).

1. What should be changed?

Is it about a merger or, alternatively, a splitting up of departments, are the total collection of job descriptions being revised, are people to be made redundant or is the organization growing instead? These are all changes in the design, the construction of the organization. If the organization already has an Enterprise Architecture worked out on basis of SqEME®, it is relatively simple to specify this change and to get a view of the impact on the operation. A reorganization can also be the reason for visualizing processes more clearly and, in doing so, to ensure that the focus remains on the key requirements during the transition to the new organizational structure. In an merger process, the joint development of the Enterprise Architecture and the Key Result Area descriptions can take care of the link between the merging partners.

---

[61] Kaplan and Norton (1999), The balanced scorecard: translating strategy into action.

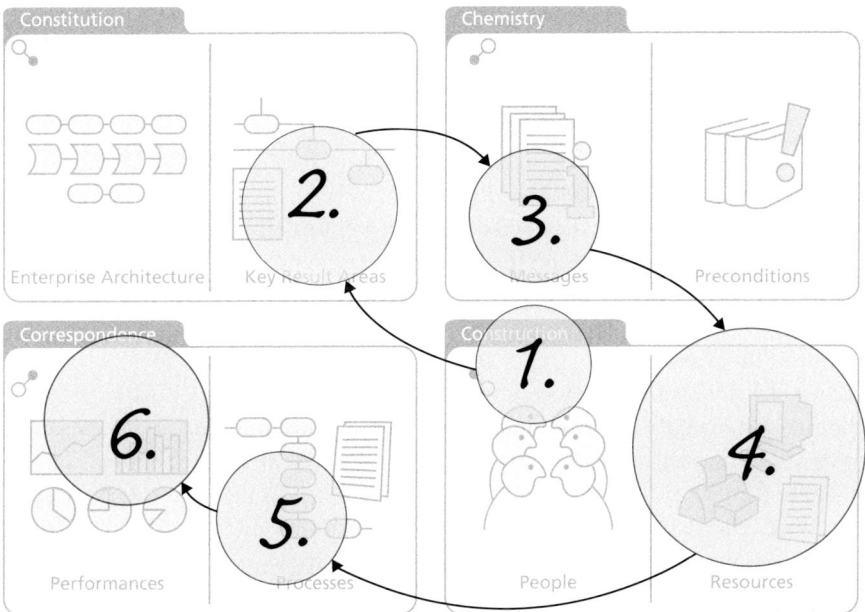

Figure 9.4   Implementing a reorganization

2. Which processes are touched by the reorganization?

In an (either new or established) Enterprise Architecture and ditto Key Result Area descriptions, it can be highlighted where the reorganization affects work. This can be done in the boardroom, or equally in one or more workshops. When it is important to emphasize the identity and collectiveness of the new organization, the latter method is preferable. The more these kind of notions arise from the collective, the less the question occurs about how to 'get the new processes into the heads of the employees'. As a result, the reorganization initiative becomes a project that is actually owned by the (new) organization.

3. How are the distribution of tasks and the internal communication influenced?

A reorganization can mean that processes will be executed in a fundamentally different way. When, for instance, the decision is taken to migrate from a decentralized to a centralized purchasing function, it has serious consequences for the division of tasks and the associated communications. If an organization decides to work in a more project-based manner, this translates into more formal messages with regard to, for instance, the project assignment, project plan, milestone reporting and final delivery document. As part of the discussions regarding Key Result Area descriptions and the message specifications underneath them, these notions can be made explicit, offering a firmer basis for managing change. Using these processes to calculate rules, assumptions and possibly simulations can provide an even better appreciation of the necessary information.

4. Which measures should be taken?

Carrying out a reorganization requires adopting the measures of change. From the discussions about the Key Result Areas, processes and messages, one can devise an action list on these construction aspects, emphasized by the Construction window of the SqEME® approach to process management. This list then presents items such as the adjustment of specific job profiles and organizing the accompanying instructions and education. The list can contain an overview of the measures that are to be taken on the subject of ICT: is it just readjusting the authorization profiles or do changes go deeper and is there a need for new ICT services?

5. What are the consequences for the processes?
With the help of process flowcharts, the desired situation can be mapped further and transferred to the employees involved. Whether the desired situation will be described just *for* or also *with* the workers in these processes, depends on the adopted strategy of change and the current style of management.

6. How to control the transition?
Through the use of a combination of process flowcharts and management information, it can be verified if the intended change actually manifests itself in the required form. To help the transition, process flowcharts and management information can be used as a check on the compliance to the reorganization plan, or rather as means of 'learning by doing'. In the latter case, it is about exploring the most suitable new organization form while the transition is already taking place. Just as in the previous step, the choice depends upon the current management style and corporate culture, and the predictability of technological developments or market trends.

Contemplation
Just as with the chicken-and-egg problem, it is possible to have a similar discussion about processes and organization: which one came first? In other words, does the organization follow the processes or is it the other way around? In the case of the SqEME® approach, we want to make clear that the essence of the organization, its constitution, is something different from how the organization has been shaped in terms of the construction. The main message is that the two aspects should match; the Constitution and the Construction. Whether a reorganization happens because it logically arises out of the process architecture, or because management has decided to for other reasons, is mainly a matter of the personal preference of senior managers. However, processes and messages can help to bring structure to the process of change.

9.5   The Organization Wants to Record the Know-how of the Employees

Sometimes, process management requires the recording of working methods in order to standardize the work, leading to the reduction of failures or disturbances. The recording of knowledge and the insight of employees in relation to work instructions and process flowcharts is important, particularly if it is about very critical work, as mistakes can have major effects, like in aviation, but also in cases where the outputs or services are difficult or even impossible to replace. Also in laboratories, Standard Operating Procedures (SOP's) are a generally accepted way of working. The questions successively asked are: which critical operations are we talking about (1), which requirements do we want these operations to meet (2), how do we organize the work in such a way that the practical execution remains within the boundaries (3) and how do we monitor the success of these measures (4)?

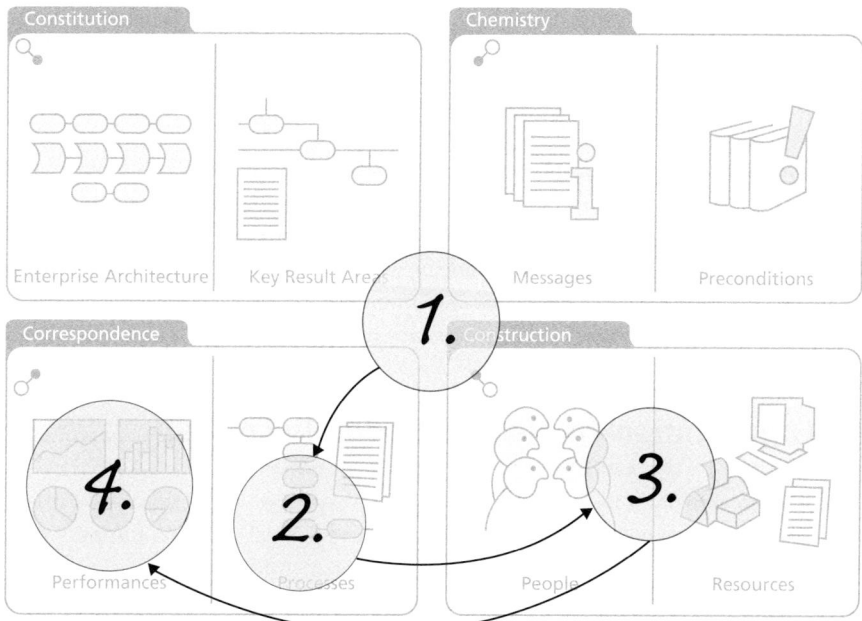

Figure 9.5   Writing down the knowledge of employees

1. What are the critical operations?

Operations can be labelled as 'critical' for various reasons. What are the effects of faults or deviations? Does the execution of the work influence the reputation of our organization, as is often the case with services? Does the work continue when senior managers are absent or do things get out of control?

2. Which requirements we set for these operations?

The desired way of working can be carefully specified based on process flowcharts. From such flowcharts one can refer to requirements of the messages and obligatory resources can be mentioned.

3. How do we implement the required way of working?

It is not always the case that ways of working, when formally documented, are actually performed this way in practice. For welding methods, the way of working is assured by a structure of welding method descriptions, welding method qualifications and welders' personal qualifications. In other organizations, one may rely on 'familiarization procedures'. Employees are expected to confirm that they have read the work orders, have understood the content and that they intend to adhere to them. Ways of operation can also be 'forced on' employees by obliging them to tick off checklists. In some cases, briefing employees in a 'toolbox-meeting' will be sufficient.

4. How do we control the compliance to procedures?

When instructing employees to follow working procedures, it becomes a question of how best to monitor and maintain these procedures. Maintaining and keeping up-to-date a system of instructions is quite an expensive affair. In practice, this accountability migrates from the line management to a specific process role, as described in section 8.7. A system of instructions can be examined for weaknesses through the use of internal auditing.

Contemplation
The development of standard operating procedures and the objective of a highly committed and professionally mature workforce actually conflict. In the SqEME® approach, the emphasis is on the assumption of craftsmanship, or better, the professional maturity of the worker. This does not exclude the necessity for a system based on working procedures because of legislation or high risks, like in the air transport. Be clear about the importance of this in the organization and by explaining this, demonstrate the respect for the professionalism of the employees.

9.6   The Organization Wants to be More 'In Control'

When an organization adheres to the principle 'to measure is to know', this leads to investment in the management information system, a 'data warehouse' and the realisation of, for instance, a Business Balanced Scorecard.

When working on gaining control of the processes from these perspectives, the key questions are: what are the critical success factors in our processes (1), how can we measure them (2), who takes control (3), how will the measurements take place (4), and how, and to whom, will we report the management information (5)? Illustrated as a journey along the windows, it provides the picture as shown in figure 9.6.

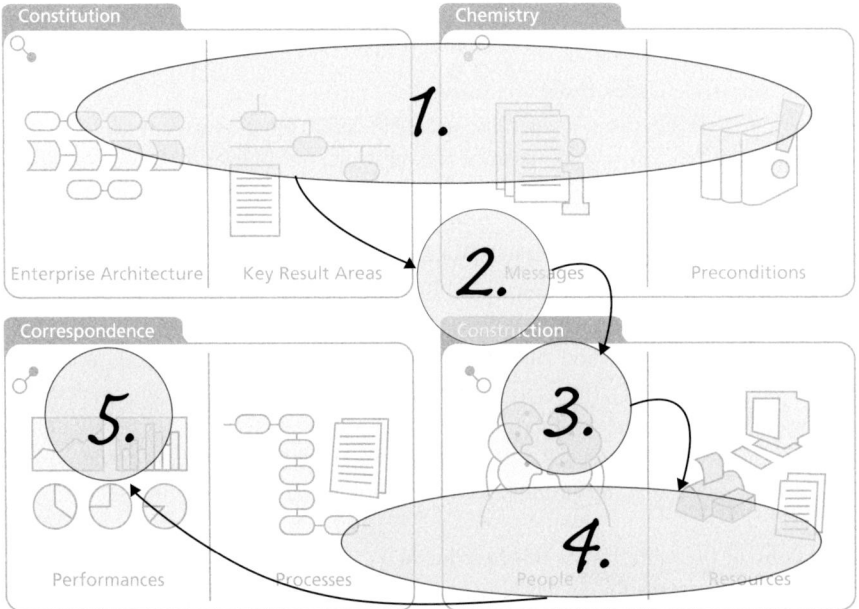

Figure 9.6   The organization wants to get 'in control'

The step-by step plan shows many similarities to the scenario concerned with getting more attention for continuous improvement, illustrated in section 9.3. The issue of 'control' requires special attention for the message specifications. Based on the messages one can, for instance, unambiguously measure timeframes. The messages are like the 'croquet wickets' of the business processes and, for that reason, are very useful points of measurement in the process.

Furthermore, the difference from the 'continuous improvement' scenario is particularly in the 'mindset' of the senior managers. Is the organization managed on a basis of confidence and is management information the starting point for improving the quality of processes, or does management information focus more upon control, accountability and settlement? The pattern in the windows is the same for both to a large extent, only the perception of the shared values is different.

9.7 The Organization Wants to Cooperate Better with its Supply Chain Partners

Exploring the potential for cooperation with supply chain partners means: discovering mutual interests (1), exploring the possibilities of working more closely together(2), determining what this means for the interaction with clients, suppliers and other stakeholders (3), analysing the consequences for the internal working procedures (4), and deciding what investments should be made for this (5).

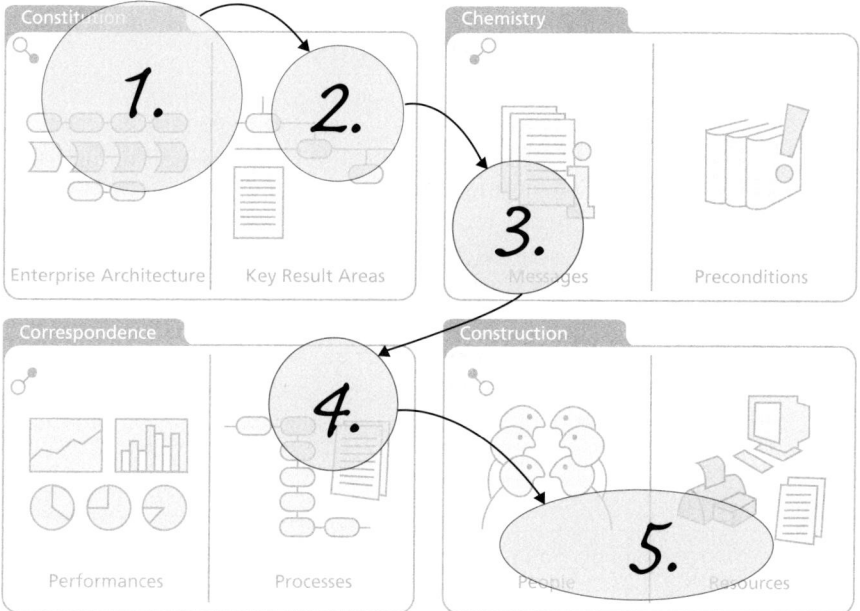

Figure 9.7   Cooperation with supply chain partners

What catches the eye is that a scenario like this starts with the belief that the search for mutual interests will pay off in the long run. The project as illustrated does not end with a view through the Correspondence window, but with an overview of investments that are expected to be profitable on the long term. In general these projects will, of course, be judged thoroughly on their result.

Constitution. With the Enterprise Architecture one looks at dependencies, or other forms of cooperation, for more intensive or different forms of cooperation. For example, a question at the level of the Enterprise Architecture is: 'Why do we not outsource all our maintenance activities?' Considerations like this lead to a discussion on the present way of managing the Key Result Areas.

Chemistry. The changes in the design of these Key Result Areas lead to other communication patterns and constituent messages. For example: When one decides to outsource all maintenance activities, the information will also flow differently.

Correspondence. Planning processes and, for example, purchase processes have to be readjusted.

Construction. These things have consequences for the division of tasks and the work instructions and may lead to new, or adapted ICT, and to (re)education of employees.

Contemplation
To get a view at what binds supply chain partners, it is conceivable to make a process model of the supply chain: in effect a supply chain model that is a composition of the Enterprise Architectures of the individual supply chain partners. In the public sector, for example the criminal justice value chain or the value chain of employment and income, there has been investment in the development of models like this for the purpose of value chain automation projects.

9.8   The Organization Wants to Renew its ICT

Information management and process management are closely linked together. ICT projects don't, however, necessarily start from the need to improve processes or to improve the interaction between processes and professionals. In some instances ICT just needs to be replaced because the technology has outdated and is not supported any more. The start point, therefore, is the notion that specific ICT needs to be replaced, improved or newly implemented (1). One can deduce from the functionality of the old and new ICT which messages this is going to have consequences for (2) and how this will influence the coherence of processes (3). When a resultant description has been distilled of the changes in the existing ways of working that will result from the new or the adapted ICT (4), the transition to the new situation can be assessed in its full magnitude and then planned. The benefits arising out of the investment in ICT will be measurable in tangible terms(5).

Contemplations
The world of ICT is changing rapidly. An important development is that the concept of ICT as 'computer systems' or 'ERP systems' is gradually changing towards ICT being 'IT services'. This movement is fundamental. It provides a completely different view of the way ICT can be deployed in organizations. Using the term 'Software as a Service' (SaaS), a whole new way of handling and using ICT manifests itself. One in which the user, the worker in the organization, becomes much more centralized. This migration from systems to services matches the developments and

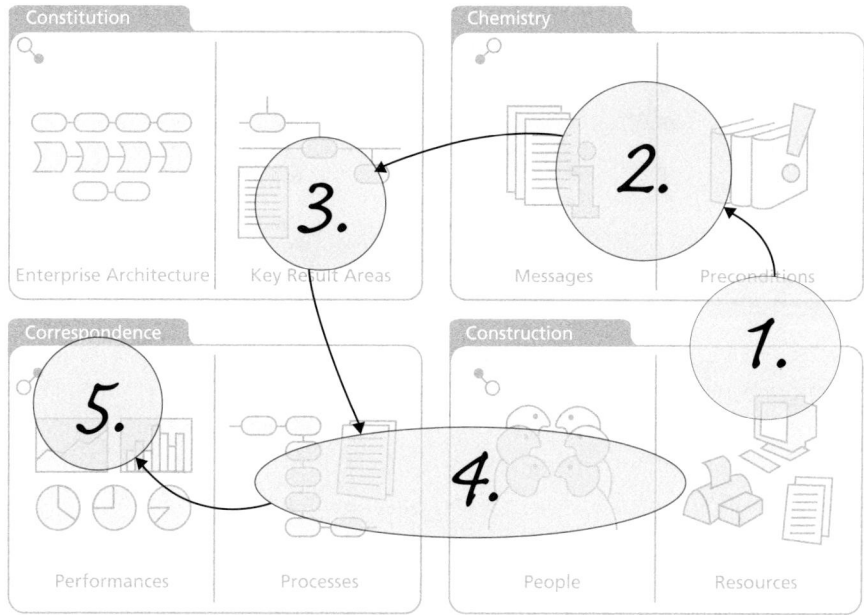

Figure 9.8   Renewal of ICT

the concepts illustrated in the introduction to this book. Where organizations become more and more dependent of the quality of the individual employee, IT services will provide them with the right information at the right time.

'Services', a different paradigm with respect to ICT
An important challenge for the current ICT is to define these IT services, to develop and to implement them. With process management, organizations are doggedly searching for more coherence in their processes. Mapping the way of working in the organization, between the organizations and between customer and organization enables these services to become more explicit and will intensify the demand. The so-called 'island automation' offers too little coherence and flexibility for the modern day requirements. Systems are, by definition, compartmentalized and offer people too little opportunity to cooperate. Because many computer applications all contain their own data of, for instance, clients or products, this poses the threat of redundancy or offers the potential to share data and information. Through growing 'process awareness' in organizations, together with the demand for coherence and the increasing willingness to cooperate, the potential benefits and associated demand for introducing ICT have moved to a higher plane: we are seeing information supply for uniting professionals. This balance between system and professional appears to have not been found yet in many organizations.

Thinking in 'services' actually means a change of paradigm. By thinking in 'services', ICT leaves the reference framework of 'old bookkeepers thinking' that has developed and manifested itself during the twentieth century, and has proven itself very successful also. This 'old-school ICT' in many cases is used like the bookkeeper keeps his overview of finance, supplies, etc. with his card-index box. Through the use of a computer application, transactions are entered and processed as a result of filling in fields in the database. It may work conveniently, but it still follows the

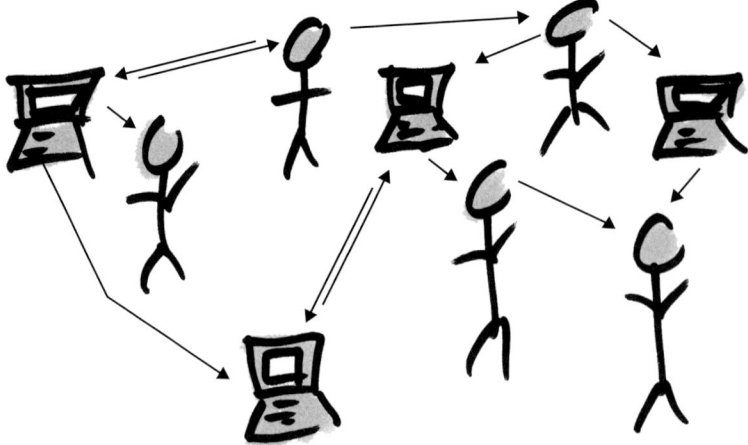

Figure 9.9   What is at the centre of the organization, the ICT or the human being?

same principle as the original card-index box: by entering the data the transaction is interpreted and this leads to an update of overviews and subsequently, through 'business rules', to initiating appropriate actions. The original transaction can usually be traced back from the rules of the database.

'ICT new style' cherishes the original transaction and stores it in the form, and with the characteristics, of an XML message. This transaction is entered into an IT service via a browser, and saved via the Enterprise Service Bus (ESB).

XML stands for eXtensible Markup Language, a standard for defining formal mark-up languages for the representation of structured data in the form of run-on type (flat text). This representation is legible for both human beings and machines. Service orientation[62] is a software architecture model, not a technology in itself. A system built according to Service Oriented Architectures (SOA) usually consists of two kinds of components. On the one hand the components offering a service, the 'services', and on the other hand the components that take care of the exchange of data between the services, the Enterprise Service Bus[63].
In ICT terms, XML messages are stateful, with metadata about the way this transaction has come about and has been validated. This is contrary to the basically stateless data held in the fields of a database.

The opportunities ICT offers us with these new techniques and concepts will have an enormous impact on the way in which organizations are designed. The techniques that are already available at this moment, allow for the storage of the original transactions and the generation of a diversity of overviews at any time and in any desirable shape. In previous times, having shut the shop, the grocer had to remove all the cash register slips and register them in his card-index box in order to

---

[62]   Service Orient or Be Doomed!: How Service Orientation Will Change Your Business (Hardcover), Jason Bloomberg & Ronald Schmelzer, 2006, John Wiley and Sons.
[63]   Source: Wikipedia

maintain the overview. Essentially, with the modern ICT, this bookkeeper's routine is no longer required. Specific IT services enable the generation of all conceivable overviews and the initiation of processes on the basis of the original and authentic (stateful) data that is available through the ESB. The original cash register slips remain available, the ways of accessing them however are limitless.

Applying services and stateful storage of data makes the application of ICT much more flexible. Also the development of the ICT organization can take place on an incremental basis, specifically defined by the end user, the professional wanting to access information.

Of course, in this development the dilemma exists, just as in the shipping trade, that the first steamboats did not reach the speed of the highly developed sailing boats for some time. However it is clear that a new paradigm has arrived. A paradigm in which an organization needs to divide their ICT facilities between taking care of their authentic business data, whilst at the same time providing the desired IT services for the professionals in the organization. With these services, the latter can record and consult data and subsequently arrange, order, compare, calculate, summarize, assess, conclude and make decisions based upon the information provided by these services.

When developing the ICT function on the basis of IT services, 'standardization' is not the main issue to worry about. This standardization has to be present in the information, in a logical data model, processed in an XML schema. On the internet you can use several websites for planning a route; in essence, you are using IT services. It is perfectly possible that some of these sites make use of the same authentic data. The difference is in the 'look and feel' of the IT service; this is what determines someone's preference. This principle is equally valid for the organization of ICT. The planning of production can then be done with a variety of IT services that may even come from different manufacturers. Which one to use is down to the personal preference of the professional planner, as long as the IT services handle the business data according to the company's rules. Therefore conformity is ensured at data level. Anyone using a PDA to read their business mail as if they were using their office desktop computer already works with this concept.

Applying 'services thinking' in organizations
Why is this ICT development so important for process management? The answer lies in the enormous added value that can be delivered if the worlds of ICT and process management are able to meet. The worlds of process management and ICT can reinforce each other tremendously. Entrepreneurs have in mind a flexible organization and they want to be able to move quickly within and between processes. However this happens in a completely different way to the reference framework of the ICT specialist. The difference lies between the ICT technique and the business view on organizations

One increasingly sees the same concepts reoccurring, sometimes grouped together to form an architecture. Often the terms used have a completely different meaning for the different disciplines. For example, this is the case with the term 'process'. A master in business administration primarily thinks of the workings of one or more persons and tries to visualize the system of working, to consider processes as black boxes. For an ICT expert, a process is a series of operations that should be executed by a computer, as a triggered by the occurrence of an 'event'. For the design and the implementation of this process, ICT experts for example make use of BPEL, Business Process Execution Language. This is a type of modelling that originates from a technical system perspective, and which considers processes fully predictable: a 'white box' approach.

These days, the role of the ICT expert is anything but enviable. On one hand they get confronted with this shift of paradigm. Putting the workers at the centre of the universe, the uncoupling of IT services and data, together with a variety of new three-letter abbreviations like XML, SOA and ESB. On the other hand in many organizations, due to costs that have got out of hand and process improvements that have not been achieved, the management of ICT struggles with the question of how a process-driven organization expresses their need for ICT best. Jammed between these two issues, ICT experts are expected to deliver quantifiable improvements, preferably today. The fact that ICT still meets the desires of the user to varying or lesser degrees is often the result of the pragmatic and proactive attitude of the ICT workers themselves. They often go and have a look at how the work actually is being done and translate their knowledge into the systems requirements. Process improvements or new views of the organization are also introduced with the systems, with the risk of the mechanic taking the place of the driver.

ICT workers complain about the lack of understanding from senior management regarding such developments: 'We are busy with services and they don't even know or care about it!', 'they' referring to the supervisors in the organization, their principals. The key is that these possibilities are all under the hood. The driver of the car usually is simply not interested in this. The complaint is only justified is the organization is not able to define their processes and to make the demand for information supply sufficiently explicit. In that case the potential of ICT will be insufficiently utilized. The result can be that the ICT worker remains obliged to choose the role of driver of the car, with all its drawbacks.

By considering an organization primarily as a bundling of coherent processes, the SqEME® approach perfectly matches the notions behind the concept of 'Software as a Service'. The slogan 'Business as a Service' (BaaS) is itself a very neat description of the motto of the SqEME® approach to process management. To bridge the gap between the ICT world and those managing the business, business process management methods like SqEME® have to be founded on a social system perspective instead of a technical system perspective, emphasizing the necessity for specifying the information needs of professionals. This ultimately enables the utilization of modern ICT concepts and technical possibilities! At this moment in time, many organizations invest significantly in matching the interests of business and ICT professionals and in the development of a mutual understanding. The SqEME® foundation and the network partners have also put this issue high on their agenda. In the Construction window, ICT is of major importance and, therefore, so is communication with ICT experts. Through its network partners, SqEME® is represented on a working group of 'The Open Group', namely the one labelled with Enterprise Business Architecture, with a view to developing a coherent approach and building a bridge between the domains of process management and information management.

---

64 Hammer and Champy (1993), Reengineering the Corporation: A Manifesto for Business Revolution.

9.9 The Organization Wants to Reengineer Their Business Processes

After dealing with the eight scenarios and exploring what ICT can deliver in the future, some managers might be inclined to start all over again[64]. This ninth and last scenario is an expression of that. How would we design the organization if we were allowed to do it all over again and start from scratch? We would subsequently address the following questions:

1. What is our mission and vision?
2. Which processes, verbs, are associated with that?
3. What is the coherence between these processes?
4. What interaction is desired between these processes?
5. Which requirement should the processes demonstrably have to comply with?
6. To whom are we going to assign the activities?
7. What is necessary for carrying out these processes?
8. How can we keep track of things?

The typical idealized journey along the four windows essentially looks like that described below, starting at the upper left, going round clockwise till we arrive at the Correspondence window.

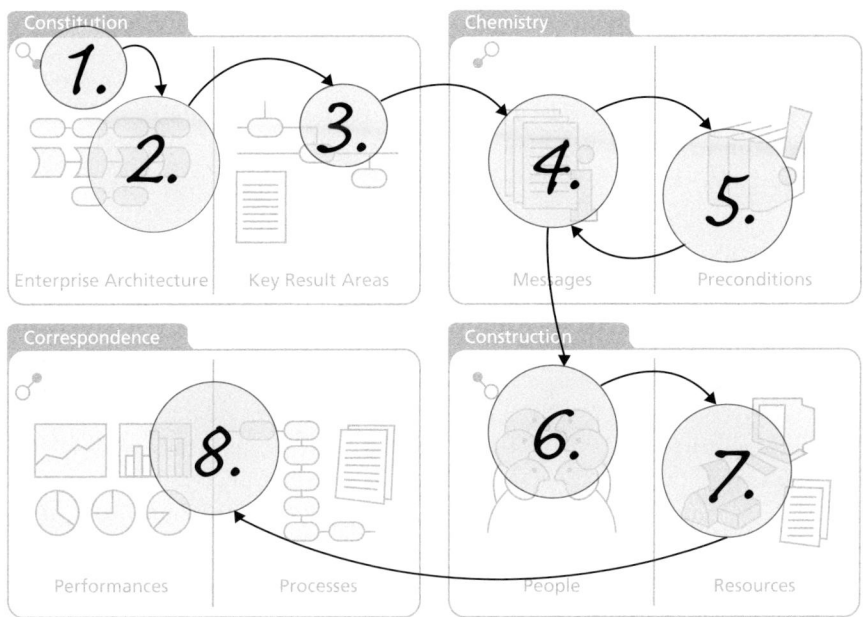

Figure 9.10   'Business Process Reengineering'

In the meantime, practice has demonstrated that re-engineering projects are based on too little respect for the history of an organization and take too little account of the smart solutions and pragmatic 'work-arounds' that have been developed during that period. The ambition to

---

[64] Hammer and Champy (1993), Reengineering the Corporation: A Manifesto for Business Revolution.

finally do it right' should increasingly require a more modest approach of 'incremental renewal'. Improve in small steps and preserve the good.

The realizing of a series of projects as in the scenario described in section 9.2, or the investment in the self-learning abilities of the organization as illustrated in section 9.3 both result in less disturbance to the daily work activities and in the long term not only yield tangible improvements but also create an organization in which working on such improvements becomes the norm. In addition, it is easier in small projects to take account of burning issues, dilemmas and priorities. The harsh reality of life is accepted as the context within which the progress has to be accomplished. Because this reality is always capable of surprising an organization and its (process) managers, the final chapter will, in addition to the scenarios outlined here, provide a checklist with points of attention for each segment of the different windows

10 The SqEME® Approach and the Harsh Realities of Life

In practice, several issues are at stake in an organization at any one time. Reality can be stubborn. Besides, the fact that simple problems appear to be more complex when looked at closely means that there is always more than one interest to be found in organizations. No single scenario will exactly suit an organization. The scenarios are meant to give an idea about the application of knowledge, the overview and the tools offered by the SqEME® approach to processes. A scenario indicates a particular way of viewing and which window dominates for a certain question. However, the application of these windows is based upon the fact that you can switch continuously between the use of the four windows. More than that, when doing so, the benefits of the SqEME® approach to process management are fully realized.

Think of the famous Ryoanji temple of the Rinzai sect in Kyoto, Japan. To this temple belongs the famous Zen garden, made of gravel and built with small islands and little rock formations. From a number of galleries one can quietly look at the garden. The peculiarity of this garden is that it consists of fifteen rocks, but this fact can only be figured out when the garden is viewed from different angles. Regardless of the angle one chooses, there are always just fourteen of these rocks visible at the same time.

This analogy makes it clear how important it is to continuously alternate the way of looking at the organization, always involving the other windows when considering specific issues. The following sections illustrate the separate use of the several windows and their parts in applying the SqEME® approach in a step-by-step fashion.

This is why we deal with the four windows again and summarize things per window after the nine example scenarios have been covered. As far as general activities are concerned, we describe how looking through one of the windows, can help you to invest in the processes and we explain the links with the points of view as seen through the other windows.

To conclude this chapter we consider the use of supporting software when applying the SqEME® approach to process management.

10.1 Encore with Points of Attention

Below, an encore follows. It is derived from daily practice and presents points of attention in relation to the respective parts of the four windows.

Enterprise Architecture
Drawing up the Enterprise Architecture can be the starting point and/or the final piece of a discussion about the essence of management.
- As a starting point, the Enterprise Architecture can come about as a result of an inventory of critical points in the business process. By clustering these, and by also assigning the critical

performance indicators to process owners, almost automatically a model appears that divides the business process into separate Key Result Areas. In a real process-driven organization the Enterprise Architecture has the same function as the well known organization chart, but it has a totally different orientation!

- The Enterprise Architecture is sometimes used as a kind of primary page, index or overview map of several Key Result Area descriptions. In such cases the Enterprise Architecture is developed afterwards for the purpose of establishing the overview, positioning and demarcation of the Key Result Areas described earlier.

It is expressly stated that an Enterprise Architecture never can be right or wrong. The model reflects how management perceive the business processes and which parts of this processes they wish to manage.

Key Result Area descriptions

The mapping of Key Result Area interaction diagrams is similar to solving puzzles with the building blocks of a demarcated piece of the business. The Key Result Area descriptions are meant to provide a coherent description of processes and messages.

Make an inventory of the content and demarcation of the Key Result Area by:
1. Describing a global, all-embracing objective of the Key Result Area. For example, for the 'Maintenance of material' the objective could be described as 'To achieve that the material can be employed according to the planning'.
2. Nominating the messages that are outgoing, controlling and incoming for the Key Result Area as a whole. This creates an unambiguous demarcation of the Key Result Area that is to be described.
3. Drawing up an inventory of the names of processes that are part of this Key Result Area by means of a brainstorm.
4. Drawing up an inventory of all relevant messages that control or monitor the information supply in daily practice from memory or by document studies.

Then produce the Key Result Area description from this inventory and from discussions with experts. This activity has several iteration cycles that gradually shorten the list of processes and messages. Try to find the similarities rather than the differences.

- During the discussion it usually turns out that the experts involved use different terms to indicate processes and messages, though they actually mean the same.
- In many cases it is also becomes apparent that the diversity of documents found in practice can be reduced by means of more simple messaging.
- Finalize the description of the Key Result Area once it has been agreed that it has been captured 'properly enough' in the diagram. This is the case if all involved persons think that the important activities and messages of the Key Result Area have been identified and represented in a logical manner.
- After this, perform a check on the consistency between the Key Result Areas. Check whether the source and destination of the messages that refer to other Key Result Areas actually match the way it is mentioned in these descriptions.

Message specification

Because the quality of information supply is a spearhead of the SqEME® method, the message specification is also an important binding element in the whole of modelling conventions. The importance of an unambiguous specification of the communication doesn't need further explanation!

- The objective and the minimum data content of the message specification are often filled in as further work is carried out into the details of a Key Result Area description. At the moment that a discussion on a Key Result Area description arrives at a deadlock, it is very enlightening to check what the people involved have in mind in relation to a specific message, for which you can be guided by the objective and the minimal data. Also, under the heading of 'remarks', lots of clarifications can be noted. Finally, one has to make absolutely sure whether the information needs and the requirement to demonstrate compliance with boundary conditions are assured by the minimal data.
- Filling in the section 'document control' is a specialist job, in which the applicable preconditions should be taken into account; this might include requirements on the subject of privacy and the specific preferences of the people involved in undertaking the process.
- If the process architecture is the starting point of an automation project, it is important that the message specifications are reviewed ('sharpened') by information analysts and process experts. These people can ensure consistency in the reproduction of the minimal data.

For instance, in the police force it makes a significant difference as to whether the message specifications speak of an offender or about a suspect. Also on the matter of document control, specialists on documents and information control can make a useful contribution. See also section 5.3 about UDEF.

Preconditions

The preconditions indicate the internal and external requirements that an organization wants or has to meet. It is of major interest to know all relevant boundary conditions and to link these to the associated messages.

- In the first place it is important that an organization knows the boundary conditions that are enforced by the market on their business management. This is a part of the responsibility of any organization, just as every citizen is expected to know the law. An organization handling this in a professional way wil have mapped all applicable internal and external preconditions.
- For specific assurance projects, the creation of a preconditions/messages matrix is the next step. Following on from this, the level to which an organization meets the applicable preconditions can be estimated. Potential gaps in the business process can then be unambiguously established and the work to 'repair' them can be accurately planned, guided by this matrix.
- In projects where investment in the process architecture is agreed on the basis of the need to improve the business, drawing up and completing a preconditions / messages matrix is a control measure to ensure that when implementing improvements, all preconditions are taken into account.

Process flowchart

Process flowcharts can be established as a result of the need to communicate the essence of the Key Result Area descriptions that have already been developed to larger groups of employees and to have them evaluated by them (see figure 10.1). The direction of development is then from large (looking at processes generally) to small (considering a single process exclusively).

Process flowcharts can also be created from the need to get an idea of the essence of one single process, that is initially isolated from the larger whole (see figure 10.2).

The movement from large to small requires that the demarcation, indicated by incoming, outgoing and controlling messages, is already known in order to develop process flowcharts.

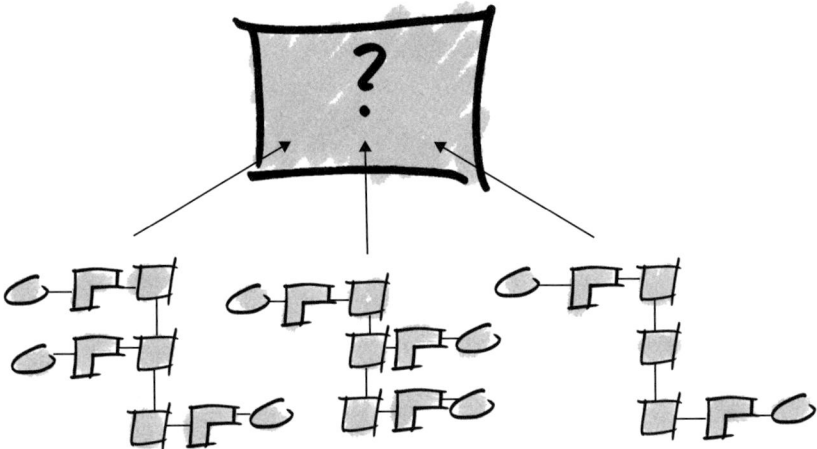

Figure 10.1   Zooming in on the process details from the whole

- In a brainstorm all conceivable activities of the process are listed.
- A process flowchart is then drawn without the middle column, but with the incoming and outgoing messages including connectors in a logical order, corresponding with the information from the Key Result Area interaction diagram.
- Consequently, the listed activities are put in logical order so that they connect the building blocks between the incoming and outgoing messages until the group agrees that a recognizable description of the process in question has been developed.
- To finalize things, in conjunction with the people involved and responsible for overseeing the process, a decision is taken on whether any incoming or outgoing messages have been forgotten. If there are any, they are drawn in and the activity diagrams, in turn, have to be completed with the missing interactions.

If the focus is upon the development of a process flowchart reflecting a movement from large to small, a different way of working is required.
- To begin with, one determines, as far as the process to be mapped is concerned, which message will complete the process and which message triggers the start.
- Subsequently the activities in between the final message and the initial message are defined from the end to the beginning (from the bottom to the top). If desired, a brainstorm is performed to identify all conceivable activities of the process.

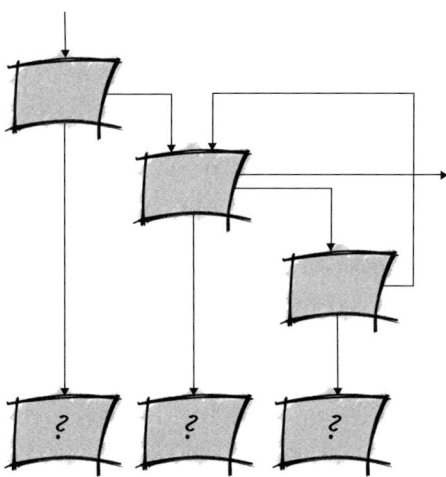

Figure 10.2   Assembling the whole on the basis of the process details

- If this way of working leads to an agreement about the flow of the process, one examines which other messages are thought to be necessary for the correct progress of the process. These messages are drawn in.
- There is also a need to examine those messages which are sent from the process to other processes or to 'outside worlds', parties outside the process . These messages are also drawn in.
- To complete things, the connectors are filled in. Depending on the view of the whole, these connectors mention other processes or refer to 'outside worlds'. During the final presentation of the process flowcharts, one ore two sentences of text may be added for clarification to both approaches. This increases the recognisability of the process flowchart and reduces the risk of miscommunication to a minimum.

Key Result Area interaction diagrams or process flowcharts?
The question is whether descriptions of Key Result Areas should be extensively and widely evaluated and agreed upon in an organization. In many cases these descriptions are too abstract to really appeal (to everyone). In general, it is more beneficial to arrive at the result by means of the Correspondence window. Process flowcharts are more appealing representations than the activity diagrams that explain the Key Result Areas. Discussions about, and comments on, such process flowcharts can lead to very useful re-adjustments of Key Result Area descriptions. Closer study of this can, in turn, lead to new insights concerning the Constitution. The Construction window offers specific assistance for the implementation of Constitution window principles. This provides something to grasp hold of when developing and implementing necessary resources in order to enable the people in the organization to perform their work to their (mutual) satisfaction.

Performance criteria
Performance criteria form the basic elements by which management can determine whether the quality of the business process is within the bounds of acceptability. Often it is quite a task to decide on the key performance indicators that enable an adequate and timely reaction to an imbalance in the performance of the business process. This is about the indicators that visualize

the operation of the business management/processes. For example, the process time that passes between the request for a quotation from a client and the actual ordering of the goods or services. In this case, it is not about the type of indicators that are often available in management reports, like for instance the gross margin. That indicator is derived from a set of constituent performance indicators.

- Guided by the mission, vision and operational strategy, define the dominant issues of the organization and their leaders.
- Investigate which processes seem to relate to the defined issues.
- Select those processes that, after careful investigation of the available management information, can be assumed to influence the dominant issues.
- For instance, investigate what are the key success factors in the field of the dominant issues by means of fishbone diagrams.
- In relation to the processes, identify those performance indicators that correlate with the success factors and establish ways in which they can be measured.
- Sort out all performance indicators for the dominant issues and verify whether a balanced perception appears of the performance of the business process.
- Because the dominant issues of tomorrow are different from those of today, it is important to review the defined set of performance indicators on a regular basis.

People
When mapping the business process, initially the Key Result Areas or processes are divided among a number of people in the organization. In many cases this distribution roughly matches the final matrix or matrices that link process responsibilities to Key Result Areas, processes or messages. During the development of the complete process architecture, the view of the business process will get increasingly subtle, and opinions and demarcation of the tasks of process owners will 'grow along'. To ensure progress in describing the Key Result Areas and processes it is important that these activities are not disturbed by Construction window discussions about 'who does what', 'who is responsible' and 'how do we do that' or 'how should we do that'. These debates can be performed efficiently at the moment that processes and messages have been worked out unambiguously, lead by the Constitution and the Construction windows. For this, it is necessary to separate the actors/messages matrix explicitly and regard it as a separate activity.

When departing from the detailed Key Result Area interaction diagrams and message specifications, the assignment of the roles 'drafting', 'checking', 'authorizing', 'taking action' and 'archiving' to the actors in the organization is a simple job. The choices with regard to the resources have an influence on these assignments. The development and implementation of changed resources can be of influence upon the existing division of tasks. Formally organizing the management of preconditions, performance criteria and resources by explicitly assigning them to people in the organization is useful if the complexity of the organization absolutely requires assignment of people other than the process managers mentioned earlier. The total of all matrix relationships between the actors in the organization and messages, processes, resources, etc. needs to be consistent with the related job description. Nevertheless, an organization needs to posses both this type of process descriptions and job descriptions. The process architecture is directed in particular at coherence in Key Result Areas and the delegation of authority, whereas a job description has its value in acquiring, assuring and rewarding the desired professionalism in the organization!

Resources

The thing the people in the organization specifically notice about the process architecture is the way their work is 'kept on track' by resources. The mapping of these resources can arise from the need to assure, to demonstrate how the work is 'under control'. The process architecture can also be used as a means to obtain the improvement and renewal of existing resources. These two different paradigms –'control' versus 'improvement'– determine whether:

- one starts with an inventory of the existing resources in order to complete the whole process architecture, or
- the message specifications and the relationships to the actors serve as a functional specification for the development of improved or new resources.

In other words, if you opt to map the present situation, then the existing resources form the starting point. The difference between the present situation and a desired situation, in which the performance is improves, is frequently found discussing the possibilities for the use of other resources: smarter solutions for getting the work done.

General hints

Experience proves that the complex process of structuring business process does not go as smoothly as planned in every situation. So, in conclusion, some hints are provided:

The rules for developing Key Result Area descriptions are simple. After one has been given a good example and some explanation, many people think they know the ins and outs. In practice, strict application proves to be more difficult. In the initial phase this requires careful guidance.

It requires a loss of habituation and practice to view processes from the SqEME® approach. Once one has internalised this view correctly, the key is letting colleagues perceive the processes the same way. This prevents a tower of Babel.

The transparency and abstraction yield a relatively simple overview of the business process, offering the best, but also the less perfect practice to rise to the surface. For the current management it can appear confrontational.

The SqEME® vision of business processes can be at odds with the ideas of management. Therefore, it is important to 'get along'. The paradigm shifts are, for example:

- from task-oriented to result-oriented;
- from functional thinking to process thinking (horizontal approach to organizing);
- from responsibility to authority;
- from exclusive to inclusive.

When looking through the Construction window, one observes the relationship between the mapped messaging of the enterprise and the people and resources that should guarantee the correct utilization of the processes.

When viewing an organization through the Chemistry window, new insights can arise about the 'constitution' of the organization (Constitution window), or about the issue of how the essence of the organization could be implemented differently (Construction window). If all these insights could really lead to better management is the answer to the puzzle laying at the desktop of the process owner. At their dashboard, the 'monitoring' of the present processes and the information supply takes place, and consideration can be given as to whether possible proposed improvements will turn out to be profitable in practice.

10.2 Use of Supporting Software

Over the last few years the use of computer applications for the development and documentation of process flowcharts has grown enormously. In the early nineties, there were only a few software tools on the market and these were mainly used to support the development and command of process flowcharts. Frequently, this meant the electronic maintenance of texts and diagrams in a word processing programme (e.g. Microsoft Word) and sometimes one used so called 'case tools' (like System Developed Workbench (SDW) from Cap Gemini), in which information was stored as both text and diagrams in a database. Communication related to process flowcharts often still took place by distributing paper handbooks. However, in recent years, the computer applications have gone through an enormous development. Today there are innumerable solutions for system development, and the management and especially the disclosure of information to users. Think, for example, of the successful application of intranet and internet in reducing the amount of handbooks.

There are several solutions that can be applied to SqEME® through the use of computers and specific applications. The starting point is that the choice of the best tool, if this exists, depends strongly on the specific company situation and the desires of the user. For the successful purchase of a tool it is important to know in advance what the tool must support. Some questions on this issue are:
- Does the tool just have to support development and management, or should it also support communication of the information to the user?
- Who do we regard as user, which models and descriptions are for whom, and how often and in what situations are these models consulted?
- Should the tool be supportive when using just one of the windows or with all of them?
- Does everything have to be recorded by one tool, or can the information of the various windows be accommodated by different ICT solutions?

At the point of selecting the supportive tool(s), it is of important to verify whether a number of objects can be identified and if a number of relationships can be made between these objects. In this way one is still able to see the objects coherently defined in the four windows in the tool.

Figure 10.3 shows the objects that are used within the four windows of SqEME®. The relationships defined between the objects are also drawn in. Appendix I reflects these relationships in the form of a schedule.

The supporting software market is moving rapidly. Recent developments are subject of regular or special meetings of the SqEME® user network group. It is certainly worthwhile checking the website www.sqeme.nl!

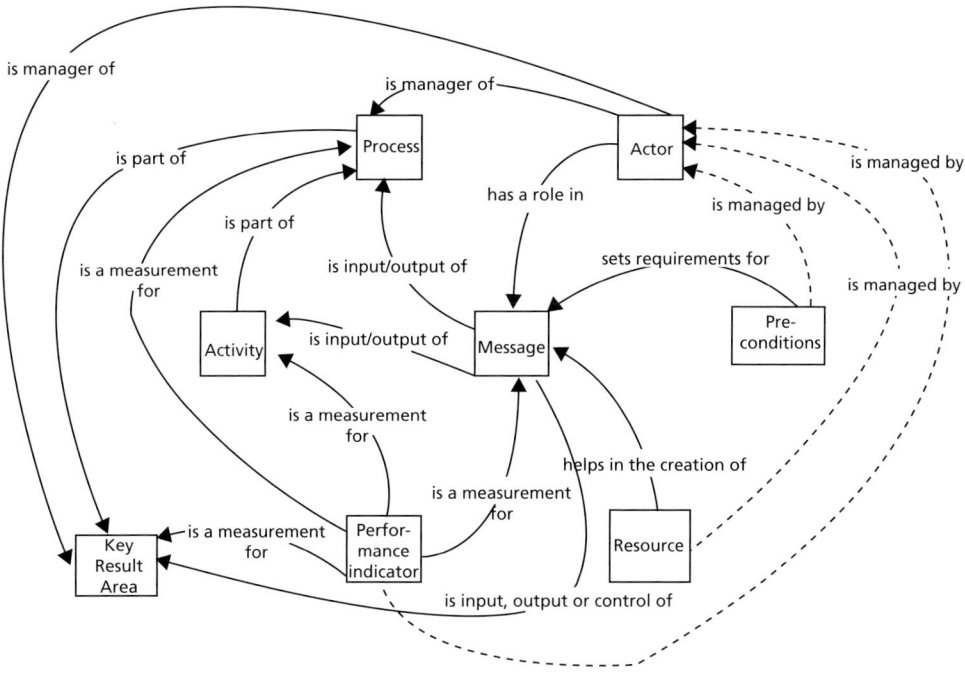

Figure 10.3   Relationships between the objects used in the windows

Appendix I   SqEME® Objects and Relationships

Process Management and the SqEME® Approach

Objects	Key Result Area	Process	Activity	Message
Properties	Interaction diagram	Flowchart	Description	Result Minimal content Remarks Document control
Relations				
Key Result Area	a business is single or composed of other functions (conventions SADT mother/child)			
process	process is part of Key Result Area	process follows or precedes another process		
activity	implicit	activity is part of a process	activity follows or precedes another activity	
message	message is input, output or control of a process	message is input or output of a process	message is input or output of an activity	a message is single or composed of other messages (with inherited properties)
actor	actor is manager of Key Result Area	actor is manager of a process	implicit	actor is drafter, checker, authorizer, customer, archivist and/or manager of a message
resource	implicit	implicit	implicit	resource helps in the creation of the message
performance indicator	performance indicator is a measurement for the quality of a Key Result Area	performance indicator is a measurement for the quality of the process	performance indicator is a measurement for the quality of the activity	performance indicator is a measurement for the quality of a message
precondition	implicit	implicit	implicit	precondition sets requirements for message

All objects have a unique name and version indicator.

actor	resource	performance indicator	precondition
Type (position/board/ assignment) Description	Description	Description Quantity Measurement method	Description
actor supervises another actor or is member of a group or has a role delegated (groups and roles are also actors, participation according to specific task)			
resource is managed by actor	a resource is single or composed of other resources		
performance indicator is managed by actor	implicit	a performance indicator is single or composed of other performance indicators	
precondition is managed by actor	implicit	implicit	a precondition is single or composed of other preconditions

Appendix II SqEME® Examples

Key Result Area interaction diagram

Subject:
Execution of operations

Objective:
To achieve that the maintenance and repair activities are performed as agreed upon with the client.

Worked out Key Result Area:

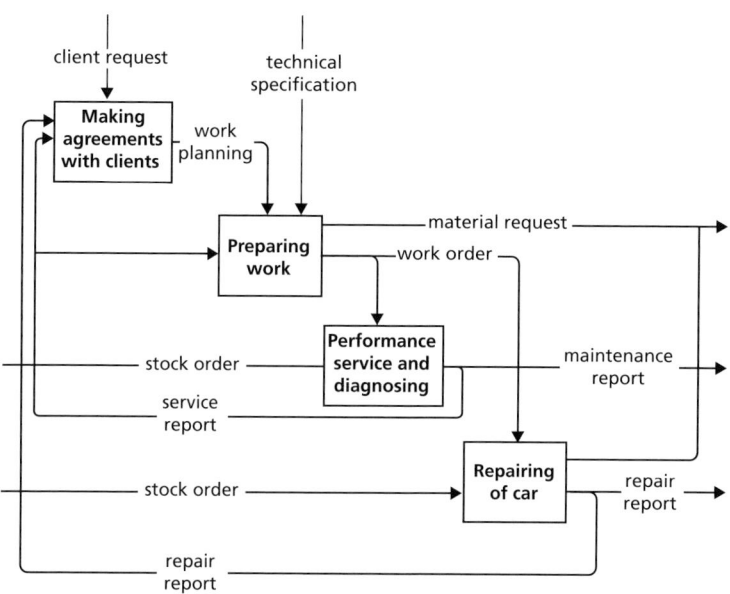

Owner of Key Result Area:
Workshop manager

Performance indicator:
n/a

Key Result Area interaction diagram

Subject:
Selling cars

Objective:
To achieve that orders are placed.

Worked out Key Result Area:

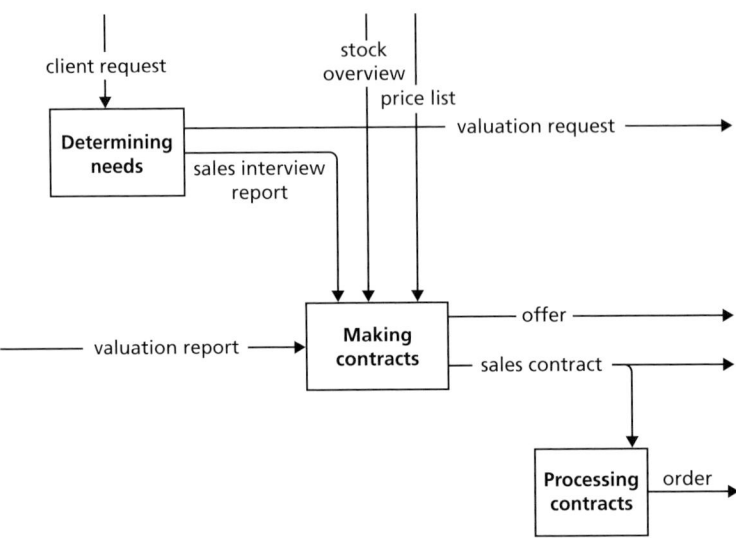

Owner of Key Result Area:
Sales manager

Performance indicator:
Order frequency (in number of orders)
Order value (in Euros)
Time to acquire (in working days)

Key Result Area interaction diagram

Subject:
Internal audits

Objective:
To achieve that an internal auditing system is operational to verify and improve on the agreed ways of working

Worked out Key Result Area:

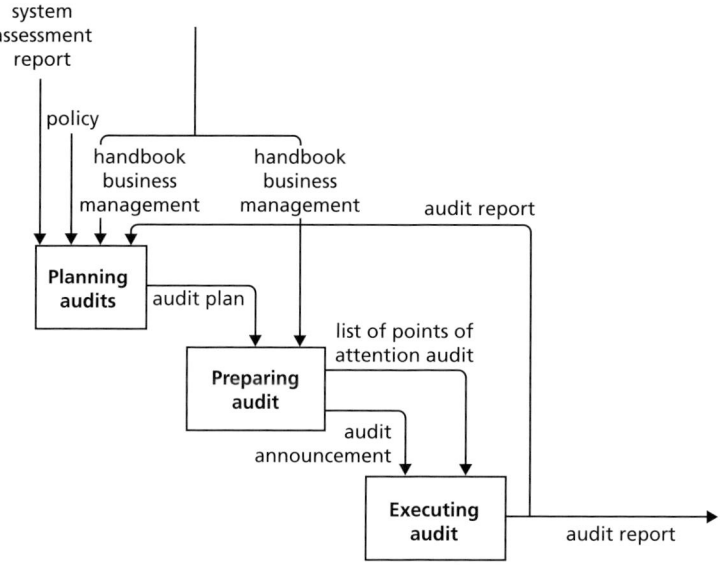

Owner of Key Result Area:
Managing director

Performance indicator:
Spent capacity (in man-hours)
Performed audits (in number of audits)
Registered deviations and improvement possibilities (in number)

Process flowchart

Process:
Preparing audits

Work out process:

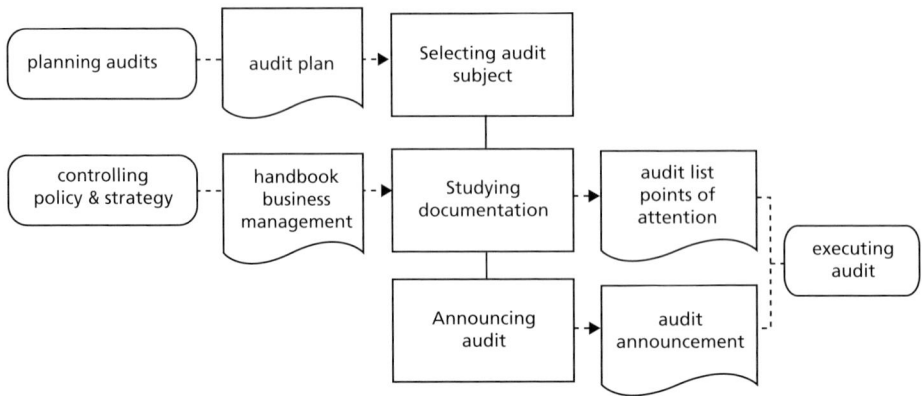

Description of activities:
Determining the audit subject
Internal audits are executed according to the pre-defined plan. In each audit a judgement is made as to whether the planned areas of interest need completion or modification.

Studying documents
One selects and studies the applicable regulations for the area of attention indicated. During the document study, the theme of the audit is detailed in the form of attention points.
During the audit, it is investigated whether these points meet the requirements and whether they deliver the right result. The sequential order is such that an efficient performance of the audit is feasible.

Announcing the audit
Every internal audit is announced formally. At the audit announcement, a copy of the list of points of interest is issued to the auditee. If the auditee is unfamiliar with auditing, the announcement is followed by a verbal explanation about the objective of auditing.

Message specification

Name message:
Maintenance report.

The result the message is about:
To achieve that the state of maintenance of the car is known.

Minimal content:
– Identification maintenance report.
– Vehicle data
  • Registration number
  • Chassis number
  • Model specification
  • Model year
  • Mileage
– Description of performed (precautionary) maintenance.
– Expenditure: time, material and equipment.
– Advice on the work to be done.

Remarks:
MOT only by certified inspector.

Document control:
Filing term 3 years (client file).

Preconditions:
–

Resources:
– Handbook maintenance checklists.
– MOT vehicle inspection form.

People:
1. Draft: Mechanic
2 Check: n/a
3. Authorize: n/a
4. Take action: Receptionist, mechanic
5. Archive: Workshop manager

Message specification

Name message:
Repair report.

The result the message is about:
To achieve that the work performed is known.

Minimal content:
– Identification repair report (work order number/date).
– Vehicle data
  • Registration number
  • Chassis number
  • Model specification
  • Model year
  • Mileage
– Description of performed work.
– Parts and materials to be debited.
– Time expenditure.
– Used equipment / applicable charges.

Remarks:
–

Document control:
Filing term 1 year.

Preconditions:
–

Resources:
Repair report form.

People:
1. Draft: Mechanic
2. Check: n/a
3. Authorize: n/a
4. Take action: Receptionist
5. Archive: Workshop manager

Message specification

Name message:
Audit attention point list.

The result the message is about:
To achieve that all persons involved in the audit are aware of the subjects under attention during the audit.

Minimal content:
– Name audit client.
– Name (names) auditee(s).
– Names auditors.
– Date, reason and subject of audit.
– Time planning.
– Points of attention
– Discussion partner per point of interest.
– Audit map.

Remarks:
–

Document control:
Filing term 1 year.

Preconditions:
NEN-EN-ISO 9001:2000 paragraph 8.2.2 Internal audit.

Resources:
Standard form 294A 'audit points of attention'

People:
1. Draft: Auditor
2. Check: n/a
3. Authorize: n/a
4. Take action: Auditor, auditee
5. Archive: Auditor

SqEME®	**Audit points of attention**	Date audit: Subject: Audit client: Page: .... of .....

Auditors:	Auditee(s):

Planning:	Points of attention	Conversation with:	Audit map

Mark the items dealt with by means of a text marker
Green = dealt with and no remarks
Blue = see notes and/or form 'Audit findings'

Standard form 294A 'Points of attention audit'

Message specification

Name message:
Job specification.

The result the message is about:
To achieve that the extent and qualifications of a position are specified.

Minimal content:
– Name position (including position code).
– Objective of the position.
– Place of the position in the organization.
– Extent of the tasks.
– Required education, knowledge, skills, medical requirements and experience.
– Responsibilities and authorities.
– Reporting obligations.
– Internal and external contacts

Remarks:
–

Document control:
Filing term 10 years.

Preconditions:
NEN-EN-ISO 9001:2000 paragraph 6.2.2

Resources:
Computer application 'Funorg' module 2.

People:
1. Draft: Personnel manager
2. Check: Head of department
3. Authorize: Managing director
4. Take action: Employee, head of department
5. Archive: Personnel manager

Referenced documents

Ahaus, C.T.B., Heer de A. & Swinkels, W.K.J, *ISO 9000:2000-serie, strategie en aanpak*, 2001, Kluwer Deventer, ISBN 9014068174

Ahaus, C.T.B., *Bevoegdheidsverdeling en organisatie*, 1994, (Thesis) Rijksuniversiteit Groningen / Kluwer Deventer, ISBN 9026720653

Ahaus, C.T.B., Dialoog over bevoegdheid en verantwoordelijkheid. In: *Kwaliteit in praktijk*, oktober 2005, Sigma

Batelaan, M. & Essen F., Management van meesterschap, In: *Nyenrode Management Review*, nr. 7, nov/dec 1997

Beer, S., *Diagnosing the system for organizations*, 1995, John Wiley & Sons Ltd., ISBN 0471951366

Berge, A.P. van den, et al, *Werkboek werkconferenties*, 1999, Reed Business Information, ISBN 9789059010710

Bloomberg, J. & Schmelzer, R., *Service Orient or Be Doomed: How Service Orientation Will Change Your Business*, 2006, John Wiley & Sons Inc., ISBN 9780471768586

Boerwinkel, F., *Inclusief denken*, 1966, published by Paul Brand in cooperation with Stichting Werkgroep, ISBN 9022824233

Bono, E. de, *The Mechanism of Mind*, 1969, Penguin Books, London, ISBN 0224617095

Bono, E. de, *De Bono's Thinking Course*, 1994, Facts on File, ISBN 0816031789

Bono, E. de, *Serious Creativity*, 1992, Harper Collins, ISBN 9780002157889

Bruin, H. de, *Prestatiemeting in de publieke sector*, 2006, Lemma, Utrecht, ISBN 9789059314733

Camp, P., *De kracht van de matrix*, 1997, Business Contact, Den Haag. ISBN 9789025414474

Covey, S.R., *The seven habits of highly effective people*, 1989, Simon & Schuster Inc., ISBN 9781416502494

Crosby, P.B., *Quality without Tears - the art of hassle-free management*, 1985, Plume/New American Library Trade, ISBN 9780452263987

Davenport, T. H. & Short, J.E., The New Industrial Engineering: Information Technology and Business Process Redesign, In: *Sloan Management Review*, 1990, 31(4) : pp 11-27

Davenport, T.H., *Process Innovation: reengineering work through information technology*, 1993, Harvard Business School Press, Boston

Dietz, J.L.G., *DEMO, introductie tot / Een reis door kabouterland,* 1996, Samsom Bedrijfsinformatie B.V., Alphen aan den Rijn

Dietz, J.L.G., *Business Process Modelling,* 1998

Eriksson, H.E. & Penker, M., *Business Modelling with UML*, 2000, Wiley, New York.

Es, R.M. van & Post, H.A., *Dynamic Enterprise Modeling*, 1996, Kluwer Bedrijfsinformatie B.V., Deventer

Esch, P.J.M. van, *Kwaliteit & Service,* 1991, Uitgeverij Veen, Amsterdam/Antwerpen

Friedman, T.L., *The world is flat*, 2006, Penguin book, Londen

Galbraith, J.R., *Designing complex organizations,* 1973, Addison-Wesley

Goldfarb, H.E. & Prescord, P.,*The XML Handbook*, 1998, Prentice Hall PTR, Upper Saddle River

Guinta, L.R. & Praizler, N.C., *The QFD Book*, 1993 Amacom Books, New York

Hammer, M., Reengineering Work: Don't Automate, Obliterate, In: *Harvard Business Review*, july/augus 1990: pp. 104-112

Hammer, M. & Champy, J., *Reengineering the Corporation: A Manifesto for Business Revolution* 1993,, Harper Business

Hammer, M. & Stanton, S., How Process Enterprises Really Work, In: *Harvard Business Review*, nov/dec 1999, pp. 108-118

Hardjono, T.W., *Ritmiek en organisatiedynamiek,* 1997, Kluwer Bedrijfsinformatie, Deventer

Hardjono, T.W., *Kwaliteitsmanagement; laveren tussen rekkelijken en preciezen, op zoek naar mumsels, oratie, 1999.*

Hardjono, T.W. & Bakker R.J.M., *Management van processen*, 2006, Kluwer Deventer

Hardjono, T.W., S. ten Have & ten Have W.D., *The European Way to Excellence*, 1996, Quality Publications Ltd

Hilverdink, R. e.a., *Praktijkboek kwaliteit & bedrijfsvoering*, <u>2001</u>, WEKA, Amsterdam

Imai, M., *Kaizen - The Key to Japan's Competitive Success*, <u>1986</u>, McGraw-Hill Book Company, ISBN 9780075543329

Handreiking verbeteren en vernieuwen en Organisatieontwikkeling van fase II naar fase III, <u>2004</u>, INK publicaties, www.ink.nl, Zaltbommel

Jacobson, I., M. Ericsson & Jacobson, A., *The Object Advantage - Business Process Reengineering With Object technology*, <u>1999</u>, Addison-Wesley Publishing Company, New York

Juran, J.M., *Juran's Quality Control Handbook*, <u>1988</u>, McGraw-Hill Publishing Company, New York

Juran, J.M., De kwaliteitstrilogie, een universele aanpak voor kwaliteitsbeheer, Int: *Sigma*, nr. 5/6, 1986, pp 23-28

Kaplan, R.S. & Norton, D. P., *The balanced scorecard: translating strategy into action*, <u>1996</u>, Harvard, Business School, ISBN 9780875846514

Kelly K., *De spelregels voor de nieuwe economie,* In: *Ode*, nr. 17, nov/dec 1997

Kelly, K., *Out of Control*, <u>1994,</u> Addison-Wesley Publishing Company, New York

Kerklaan, L.A.F.M., *De cockpit van de organisatie,* <u>2006</u>, Kluwer, Deventer

Kosko, B., *Fuzzy Thinking*, <u>1994</u>, Flamingo, London

Larman, C., *Applying UML and Patterns*, <u>2004</u>, Pearson Education Limited, Essex

Marca, D.A. & McGowan, C.L., *Structured Analysis and Design Technique*, <u>1988</u>, McGraw-Hill Publishing Company, New York

Marks, E.A. and M. Bell, *Service Oriented Architecture*, <u>2006</u>, John Wiley & Sons, Inc., New Jersey

Mills, C.A., *Quality Audit - A Management Evaluation Tool*, <u>1989</u>, McGraw-Hill Publishing Company, New York

Mintzberg, H., *The Nature of Managerial Work* ,<u>1973</u>, Harper&Row, New York

Morgan, G., *Images Of Organization*, <u>1986</u>, Sage Publications, California

Morgan, P.S., *The unwritten rules of the game , Master Them, Shatter Them, and Break Through the Barriers to Organizational Change*, <u>1994</u>, Mac-Graw Hill, ISBN 9780070570757

Oosten, Jos. N.A van, De telewerkmanager is een procesmanager, In: *Telewerken*, nr. 4, sept 1997

Owen, H., *Open Space Technology*, 1997, Berrett-Koehler Publishers Inc., San Francisco

Peters, T., *Het einde van de hiërarchie*, 1993, Uitgeverij Contact, Amsterdam/ Antwerpen

Pirsig, R.M., *Zen and the art of motorcycle maintenance*, 1976, Bert Bakker, Amsterdam

Quinn, R.E. et al., *Becoming a master Manager*, 4th edition, 2007, McGraw-Hill, ISBN 9780470050774

Smith, H. & Fingar, P., *Business Process Management, the third wave*, 2003, Meghan-Kiffer Press, Tampa

Svantesson, I., *Mind mapping & memory*, 1990, Kogan Page Limited

Tapscott, D. & Ticoll, D., *The naked corporation*, 2003, Free Press, New York

Tepper, H.J. & Mulder, F.A., *Kwaliteitsmanagement en resultaatgerichte bedrijfvoering / RGB*, Kluwer, Deventer 2002.

The Open Group, *The Open Group architecture Framework TOGAF™ - 2007 Edition*, Van Haren Publishing, ISBN 9789087530945

Toffler, A., *The Third Wave*, 1980, Bantam Press, New York

Toffler, A., *Powershift*, 1990, Bantam Press, New York

Velzen, R.C.G. van, J.N.A. van Oosten, Th. Snijders & Hardjono, T.W., *SqEME® Procesmanagement – Taal en Tekens*, 2007, Stichting SqEME®

Vorstman, H.R., *Produktmarktbeleid en kwaliteit - relaties, rekenschap en raak vlakken*, 1991, Samsom Bedrijfsinformatie, Alphen aan den Rijn

Weick, K.E., The Social Psychology of Organizing, 1979, McGraw-Hill

Womack, J.P., D.T. Jones & Roos, D., *The Machine That Changed The World*, 1990, Rawson Associates, New York

Recommended websites

SqEME-website   www.sqeme.org
The Open Group www.opengroup.org
UDEF-info   www.opengroup.org/udefinfo/
EFQM-website   www.efqm.org
INK-website   www.ink.nl